summoned *to* LEAD

Sample Resources by Leonard Sweet

11 Genetic Gateways to Spiritual Awakening
AquaChurch
Carpe Mañana
Communication and Change in American Religious History
A Cup of Coffee at the SoulCafe
FaithQuakes
Health and Medicine in the Evangelical Tradition
Jesus Drives Me Crazy!
The Jesus Prescription for a Healthy Life
Quantum Spirituality: A Postmodern Apologetic
SoulSalsa
SoulSalsa audio
SoulTsunami
SoulTsunami audio
Strong in the Broken Places

Learn about these resources at http://www.leonardsweet.com

summoned *to* LEAD

leonard sweet

ZONDERVAN™

GRAND RAPIDS, MICHIGAN 49530 USA

We want to hear from you. Please send your comments about this book to us in care of zreview@zondervan.com. Thank you.

ZONDERVAN™

Summoned to Lead
Copyright © 2004 by Leonard I. Sweet

Requests for information should be addressed to:
Zondervan, *Grand Rapids, Michigan 49530*

Library of Congress Cataloging-in-Publication Data

Sweet, Leonard I.
    Summoned to lead / Leonard Sweet.
       p. cm.
    Includes bibliographical references and index.
    ISBN 0–310–23222-8
    1. Leadership—Religious aspects—Christianity.   I. Title.
BV4597.53.L43S94 2004
253'—dc22

2004002601

This edition printed on acid-free paper.

Scripture versions cited in this book are listed on page 6, which hereby becomes part of this copyright page.

The website addresses recommended throughout this book are offered as a resource to you. These websites are not intended in any way to be or imply an endorsement on the part of Zondervan, nor do we vouch for their content for the life of this book.

Interior design by Nancy Wilson

Printed in the United States of America

04 05 06 07 08 09 /❖ DC/ 10 9 8 7 6 5 4 3 2 1

To Caden Walker Sweet and Conor Leonard Sweet
twin pirates of the heart

Scripture versions cited in this book:

Contents

Acknowledgments

I write about things I want to learn more about.

"To be a writer does not mean to preach a truth," novelist Milan Kundera has written. "It means to *discover* a truth." In the process of "discovering" the truths of something I wanted to learn more about (leadership, the Shackleton saga), certain people helped turn my ears into eyes. Mark Wilson (Knoxville, Tennessee), Jason Minnix (Portland, Oregon), and Terry O'Casey (Warrenton, Oregon) read early drafts of the manuscript and pointed out numerous places where I had a fair eye but a tin ear. Mary Kate Morse's encouragement kept me on course, even when I wanted to abandon ship. Paul Woods and Jim Ruark gave invaluable editorial assistance in keeping the "modulations" on track and reminding me that the reader does not want to know everything that the author knows.

My research assistant Betty O'Brien prevented many less head-on collisions with my subject matter than are already here. Many times Betty led me by the ear to hear the music and to face the Music. The care and ingenuity of my executive assistant, Lyn Stuntebeck, enabled me to compose on the hoof while speaking at ports of call around the world. I thank David R. Wilson and Dave Fleming for bunging down a few ideas with me. My friend Jesse Caldwell III set me straight on numerous occasions.

Inevitably, regrettably . . . "Oh, no, is this another butt-sit day?" Elizabeth, Thane, Soren, and Egil keep teaching me what it means to live under the gaze and grace of God.

This book integrates and consolidates research done over the past two decades, most of which shows up here for the first time but some of which appeared earlier in stray asides and some other guises—in an issue of my spirituality newsletter

SoulCafe, in segments of chapters in *11 Genetic Gateways to a Spiritual Awakening* (Abingdon), chapter 6 of *A Cup of Coffee at the SoulCafe* (Broadman & Holman), and chapter 5 of *Aqua-Church* (Group Publishing). I want to thank the publishers of these books for their patience with my alien registers, as well as the numerous "hearers" who for the past 15 years have put up with my discordant public lectures on "Sound Theology" and "Ultrasound Leadership" and "Sonograms of the Future," pressing me further with their questions and puzzlements. Unfortunately, I have not had the advantage of learning from Stephen H. Webb's *The Divine Voice: Christian Proclamation and the Theology of Sound* (2004), which appeared after this book was put to bed. I can't wait to learn from it.

Computer engineers used to talk about "the blinking twelve problem"—except they weren't talking about VCRs themselves. My "blinking twelve problem" has been lessened somewhat by doctoral students I work with at George Fox University: Rick Bartlett, Tony Blair, Doug Bryan, Jason Clark, Winn Griffin, Rick Hans, George Hemingway, Nick Howard, Todd Hunter, Randy Jumper, Eric Keck, Mike McNichols, Ken Niles, Craig Oldenburg, Kevin Rains, Rob Seewald, Rick Shrout, Dwight Spotts, David Wollenburg. They would have liked this book better if I had done for the other three senses (tongue, finger, nose) what I tried to do here for ear and eye. These synaesthetic leaders have ears that see, noses that hear, eyes that smell, etc. But they helped open all my senses to new stimulus, learning, and relearning.

Leonard Sweet
Valentine's Day 2004

UltraSound

The Era of the Ear

Faith is the daring of the soul
to go farther than it can see.

—19th-century theologian William Newton Clarke[1]

Leadership is the art of the future. A leader is one in whom the future shines through in support of the present in spite of the past.

But something is wrong in our understanding of leadership. The decades that brought us the greatest burst in leadership literature also brought us corporate scandals with Enron and World.com and Adelphia and Tyco and Global Crossing and Arthur Andersen, and they brought us President Bill "It-depends-on-what-the-meaning-of-'is'-is" Clinton. More than seven out of 10 USAmericans say they distrust CEOs of large corporations. Nearly eight of 10 expect top executives to take "improper actions" to help themselves at the expense of their companies.

THE VISION THING

What is wrong is "the vision thing." Our understanding of leadership needs to be turned upside down.

The future needs ears even more than it needs eyes.

In the literature on leadership, the eyes have it hands down. Warren G. Bennis's famous definition of leadership established the course for countless others: "the capacity to create a compelling vision and translate it into action and sustain it."[2] An adviser to heads of the largest nations and businesses in the world, Bennis is sometimes called "the godfather of leadership literature." In his 27 books Bennis introduced a new orthodoxy that made leadership into a science with its own set of rules and principles: leaders are made, not born. Anything that involves a goal (i.e., "vision") requires a leader, and everyone needs to be trained to be a leader. By the late 1990s, many of the 200,000 MBA graduates turned out every year had taken required "leadership" courses and "visioning" workshops.

No wonder the business world has made "vision" a catchword, perhaps *the* catchword of the 20th century.

It was this definition of leadership's intellectual haute couture that inserted itself into a presidential campaign. The phrase "the vision thing" stems from candidate George Bush's 1988 response to a friend who suggested that he spend some time thinking about what he would do as president.

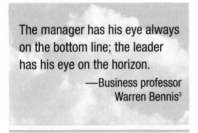

The manager has his eye always on the bottom line; the leader has his eye on the horizon.

—Business professor
Warren Bennis[3]

Bush blurted out, "Oh, the vision thing."

George W. Bush now says that what he learned from the mistakes of his father was, "The vision thing matters."[4]

His MBA-less father was right.

This is an anti-leadership leadership book. It offers a patently and passionately unfashionable stance on one of the defining issues of our day.

THE CALL

To put it bluntly: the whole leadership thing is a demented concept. Leaders are neither born nor made. Leaders are summoned. They are called into existence by circumstances. Those who rise to the occasion are leaders.

Everyone is "called" by God for some kind of mission. But sometimes the "called" are "called out" for leadership. How you manifest your mission will change throughout the course of your life. But the mission remains constant. When how you do your mission and how you make your way into the world coincide, you are living the dream life.

True, some people are born leaders. It just comes with their psychological territory. But these are few and far between.[5]

Ask any kindergarten teacher. You want to know if you're a leader? Look in back of you. Anybody following?

We're all "players" in life.

Yet sometimes life summons "players" to be "leaders." It may happen only once or twice in life. Sometimes life takes shape in such a way that a player is like the missing piece of a puzzle: the exact fit for the situation. Up to that point, the jagged pieces of your life don't seem to fit into any significant pattern. But then life calls you out and summons you forth. A player in life becomes a leader, and even "born leaders" find themselves following the summoned leader. Not accidentally, the primary language of many is "hearing the call."

One freezing Thanksgiving evening, dairy worker Guillermo Garcia was herding Holsteins toward the barn in thick coveralls and heavy rubber boots. He looked up and suddenly discovered a shoeless, shivering seven-year-old boy screaming while vomiting on the manure-stained frozen mud: "My mom! My mom!"

Unfortunately, Garcia didn't speak English. But he knew someone who knew someone who did, who called 911.

The vomiting, shoeless boy was Titus Adams. Titus had run a quarter-mile in his white socks to seek help. He and his two sisters, Tiffany and Tierra, had been riding in their mother's pickup truck on a remote road north of Greeley, Colorado. They were in their pajamas, ready to be carried in and put to bed once they got home from Thanksgiving Day at Grandma's. Titus was talking to his dad on the cell phone when his mother stretched to get the phone at the call's end. She unbuckled her seat belt, then lost control. The pickup rolled twice and ejected her through the glass of the driver's window. Tammy Adams-Hill lay unconscious and near death in 23-degree weather.

The children were strapped in. Titus unbuckled his belt and checked his sisters. Tiffany's nose was bleeding and a cut on her head was staining her blond hair. Tierra was unharmed but hysterical.

Titus knew what he had to do. He bundled coats around his sisters. He gave Tierra her pacifier. He told Tiffany to "stop crying. Stay right where you are. Don't cry. I'm going for help."

The truck doors wouldn't open, so he climbed out the window his mother was thrown from. Titus looked for her in the dark and felt his way around the truck on the ground but couldn't find her. In the distance he saw lights from a small farmhouse (a tenth of a mile away), but the lights from the dairy barn shone brighter. Titus ran toward the brighter light. It was a quarter-mile away.

Titus was a called-forth leader. He saved his mom from dying that night.

Titus was not trained to be a leader. He was born a player, not a leader. But he was summoned by a situation. He was called out by history. He became a leader by responding to the call.[6]

Will you rise to the occasion? Will you be there when life calls you forth? Will you answer the call of called-forth leadership?

What is the most desirable characteristic for a new CEO? Is it vision, or is it vigilance and good corporate governance? Lou Gerstner uttered a now-famous sentiment back in 1993: "The last thing IBM needs now is vision."[7]

In one sense, the last thing the church needs is "more vision." When Christians sing "Be Thou My Vision" we are testifying to the fact that we have all the vision we need in Jesus. Where we need help is in developing a musical ear: ears to recognize the vision that is already at work in our world, ears to hear the false notes, and ears to tune ourselves to God's Perfect Pitch, Jesus the Christ.

The need to go beyond vision is borne out by arguably the two most important leadership books of the past 25 years: Tom Peters and Bob Waterman's *In Search of Excellence* (1982) and Jim Collins and Jerry Porras's *Built to Last* (1994).[8] Peters and Collins are archrivals. Their books seem to be at opposite poles. But when the rhetorical flourishes and turf markings are stripped away, both authors emphasize the same thing: What makes a successful corporation is not a great product or a great leader, but a great culture in which people are empowered in creative goodness, innovative beauty, and unyielding truth.

It's easier to hear this in the "dowdy," calm, long-haul Collins than in the "sexy," hyperactive, make-shift Peters. For Collins, "charisma is a liability—something to be overcome, like a speech impediment."[9]

Collins is known for one primary prejudice: an enduring distrust for the concept of leadership. "I've never believed in leadership," he says. "In the 1500s, people ascribed all events they didn't understand to God. Why did the crops fail? God. Why did someone die? God. Now our all-purpose explanation is leadership. . . . We have basically lots of witchcraft, lots of religion, and very little understanding."[10]

The only thing we can say for sure about great leaders is that no two are alike. Every great leader's "greatness" is different.

According to Collins, the success of the world's best companies (what he calls "Level 5")[11] can never be truly known.

Collins talks about how one gets a giant flywheel moving. At first you start to push on it and feel as if you're making little progress at all—it's barely moving. After just one revolution, you're already tired out. But you keep pushing in the same direction. As you push, the flywheel slowly accelerates; after turning a few revolutions, it gradually gains momentum. You keep pushing, and all of a sudden you realize that the wheel is going along on its own. The heavy flywheel that had been resisting your push is now going your way. And if you keep pushing, you soon find that it's going hundreds of revolutions per minute—and pushing you.

Then Collins stops to ask the question, "What was the one big push that caused this thing to go so fast?"[12]

In *Built to Last*, the leader's personality was upstaged by the organization's personality. The culture of a corporation is what produces success, not CEOs. Jack Welch didn't make General Electric's success; GE's success made Jack Welch.[13] In recent years Collins has seemed to back off his anti-leadership tack, but not before redefining what real leadership means. It is the intentionally humble and quiet leaders who truly do make a difference. Humility can win out over more powerful organizational forces.

Even if you agree with the "leadership" concept, the world doesn't need another leadership book. At last count, there are more than 10,000 books in print that have "leadership" in the title. Is it possible to bear one more without an authorial apology or excuse? Besides, what are the differences between a book on leadership by a Christian and one by Jack Welch? How many more books can *you* read based on the same formula: Follow these principles and you will change your life. The best reaction to the appearance of another leadership principle is one of resignation—another point nicely made but another instance of missing the point.[14]

> There are way more gurus than there are new ideas.
> —Business author Michael Treacy[15]

What's more, isn't the very notion of "self-help leadership" an oxymoron, since the self-help comes in decidedly relational ways: seminars, groups, tapes, and chat rooms.

THE EARS HAVE IT

The definition of leadership as "vision" trips a variety of clichés. Leadership as "vision" has become another way of talking about exercising dominance and pushing other people around with your ideas. Governor Gray Davis of California—subsequently recalled—was toast the moment he said, early in his term, that the state legislature's job was to "implement my vision."[16] Vision has become a way of declaring dominance, of achieving alpha status and stats.

Furthermore, "vision casting" is most often nothing more than "strategic planning" board games. "Visionary" endows shopworn ideas with new roadworthiness and respectability. Even worse, when leadership development is disfigured as "the vision thing," we are teaching a dysfunctional system to leaders whose success will hinge on their ability to dismantle the very thing they've been taught.

Investing more time in the vision thing is not a good deal because it's not a good ideal, as recent events have proved. When it comes to leadership, the senses are not born equal. Leadership has more to do with the ears than with the eyes. The significance of sound is the missing chord in the literature on leadership. What matters most is not the clarity of your eyes, but the charity of your heart and the clearness of your ears.

Leadership is an acoustical art.

People from other cultures have understood this better than those in the West. The words *ear* and *wisdom* are the same in ancient Sumerian. The phenomenon of leadership always will remain misty—and always should. But failure to probe the currency of hearing as well as the currency of seeing is one reason why leadership remains one of the most studied and least understood phenomenon of the last century.

After nearly 200 pages and 7,500 citations on leadership, one report concluded that it found "no clear and unequivocal understanding of what distinguishes leaders from non-leaders, effective leaders from ineffective leaders, and effective organizations from ineffective organizations."[17] Another study of the congested analysis of leadership, having compiled 110 different definitions, concludes that "attempts to define leadership have been confusing, varied, disorganized, idiosyncratic, muddled, and, according to conventional wisdom, quite unrewarding."[18]

In all this literature on leadership, the eyes are the most recurring motif and metaphor. The eyes have not always had it, however.

For Sir Ernest Henry Shackleton, it was the ears. Called by colleagues "the greatest leader who ever came on God's earth, bar none,"[19] the Antarctic explorer Shackleton understood that leadership was more than meets the eye. To adapt Paschal: the ear has its reasons that the eye knows nothing of. The ability to find one's voice and to hear and call other voices into harmonious sound is the essence of a Shackleton-inspired definition of leadership as the acoustical art of imagining the future.

Mark Twain had a bad habit of using profanity in his speech. Twain's wife was as refined and cultured as her husband was raw and coarse. Her husband's uncouth manner of speaking offended her sensibilities, and she tried many ways of curing him of his bad habit.

> All that is true in earth or sky
> Begins and ends in music.
> —Welsh poet Vernon Watkins[20]

In desperation, she tried the shock technique. "Maybe if he hears what he sounds like and I become a sounding board, he'll be so shocked at what he hears, he'll change his ways." So when Twain came home one afternoon, she met him at the door with a stream of obscenities, throwing back at him every bad word she could remember coming from his lips.

The classical curser listened quietly until she finished, and then said: "My dear, you have the words, but not the music."

For Shackleton, it was the music that gave meaning to the words. It was the music of leadership and leadership as music that gave meaning to the leadership experience. For the music of the soul to be restored to us and our organizations, leadership needs to be seen as less a performance art (visionary, manager) than a participation art (conductor, choreographer, impresario).

This participatory understanding of "leadership" is actually more in agreement with the earliest definition of the word *lead*, which is derived from the Old English, meaning "to cause to go." As a movement word and a participatory phrase, leadership as the acoustical art of the future works whether the context is log cabin or gridiron or factory floor, laboratory or lavatory.

SHACKLETON MODULATIONS: | Ernest Shackleton's Art of Leadership

The use of Sir Ernest Shackleton as a case study in an understanding of leadership as an acoustical art enables us to explore, not what or who great leaders *are*, but what great leaders actually *do*. Unfortunately, state-of-the-art leadership is better styled state-of-the-artless leadership. This book treats leadership as an art form and employs Shackleton's legacy as a means of helping readers develop a leadership cachet and a leadership soul.

When John F. Kennedy was asked how he became a war hero, he said simply, "It was easy. They sank my boat."

Shackleton became a great leader the same way Kennedy became a war hero: his boat sank. And that was one of his expedition's kinder episodes.

Sir Henry Morton Stanley, Capt. Robert Falcon Scott, and Shackleton are notorious for making the three most radiantly nightmarish trips in the history of Western civilization.[21] The

> For scientific discovery, give me Scott; for speed and efficiency of travel, give me Amundsen; but when disaster strikes and all hope is gone, get down on your knees and pray for Shackleton.
>
> —Polar explorer Apsley Cherry-Garrard (1922)[22]

power system failure of the Apollo 13 space capsule was a bad hair day compared with Shackleton's misfortunes. Shackleton braved an awful futility that few in history have faced— a two-year pizzicato of pain with no relief in sight. If the Devil has a weather face, Shackleton went face to face with the Devil longer than anyone in history who lived to tell about it. The coldest temperature ever recorded on earth was recorded in Antarctica: *minus* 128.6 degrees Fahrenheit.

In June of 1999 a 47-year-old worker at Amundsen-Scott South Pole Station discovered a lump on her breast. Because the Antarctic winters are so severe that airplanes can't land or pick up passengers, the patient was trapped and could not obtain medical help. The National Science Foundation paid the U.S. Air Force to airlift in supplies. The "mission" was simple. It entailed flying a C–141 Starlifter seven-and-a-half hours to the South Pole, opening a cargo door in midair, and pushing out of the plane four 350-pound boxes.

What made this simple airdrop "the most challenging mission we've ever attempted in peacetime," according to mission commander Lt. Col. John Pray?[23] And why did the entire world watch with bated breath as these supplies were dropped from the sky?

The Antarctic region is more inhospitable to humans than any other place on planet Earth. Eighty-below-zero temperatures and strong winds made the opening of the cargo door dangerous and the blasts of cold air life-threatening to those pushing the boxes out of the plane. The ground crew had only seven minutes to get the supplies inside the domed station before the medicine and food supplies were ruined and they themselves frostbitten by the extreme cold.

Many decades earlier, Shackleton and his crew of 28 men were stranded in such Antarctic conditions, not for seconds or minutes, but for years. From 1914 to 1917 Shackleton led his men to safety through the harshest climate and severest conditions imaginable. In spite of a true "nuclear winter," Shackleton "never lost a man." It is known as "the greatest survival story in history."

The Greatest Leader

In 1908, Shackleton became the first explorer to come within 100 miles of the South Pole. Beaten to the pole by the Norwegian explorer Amundsen in 1911 and the English explorer Scott in 1912, Shackleton set his sights on another mission: to make it across the Antarctic continent from one side to the other. Or, as the fund-raising brochure phrased it, the expedition's mission was "to cross the Antarctic from sea to sea, securing for the British flag the honor of being the first carried across the South Polar Continent."[25]

He never made it. With less than 100 miles separating them from the continent, the group's ship became trapped in an ice pack, crushed like a cracker, and flushed down the watery void. On January 19, 1915, Shackleton and his crew became stranded in the most hostile place in the world.

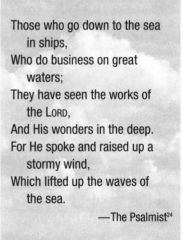

Those who go down to the sea in ships,
Who do business on great waters;
They have seen the works of the LORD,
And His wonders in the deep.
For He spoke and raised up a stormy wind,
Which lifted up the waves of the sea.

—The Psalmist[24]

So how did an "explorer" who failed in his greatest mission and never made a "discovery" ever achieve a reputation as "the greatest leader . . . bar none"? And why was his story, retold masterfully by Caroline Alexander in *The Endurance*, such a bestseller?[26]

The story of the *Endurance* expedition has a postmodern feel. Shackleton was a man clearly of his time, but a man also clearly living before his time. He combined the prophetic and priestly functions of leadership. He reached out to where his crew was (priest) and reached out to where his crew was *not* but needed to go (prophetic). He could "tell it like it is," but was willing to tell it like it is *not* but ought to be. Reaching people where they are is how leaders form relationships. But reaching people where they are *not* is how leaders form hope for "what you can be" and help construct an imaginary future toward which people can direct their steps. If "what is" is not seen in light of "what ought to be," if the priestly isn't built on the prophetic, what comes forth is the therapeutic.

Successful Failures

In postmodern culture there is a new respect for "losers" and "successful failures"—those who didn't quite achieve their dreams but generated a story in the quest. One thinks here of both institutional launches (the ocean liner *Titanic*, the spaceship Apollo 13) and individual undertakings (George Mallory and

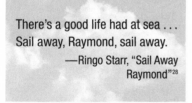

There's a good life had at sea . . .
Sail away, Raymond, sail away.
—Ringo Starr, "Sail Away Raymond"[28]

Andrew Irvine climbing Mount Everest in 1924). Shackleton stands as one of the most "splendid failures" of all time. As journalist Stephanie Capparell puts it in the *Wall Street Journal*, Shackleton "failed only at the improbable; he succeeded at the unimaginable, and is considered a model of leadership during crisis."[27]

Survivors

This is a new age of exploration. In this emerging culture, everyone is an explorer, and every profession requires sailing in uncharted waters. Hence the fascination with stories of those who explored the unknown territories of their day.

Of all exploration narratives, the ones that command the greatest attention are survivorship stories. The sheer volume of Shackleton's accomplishments as a survivor are astounding. This one Shackleton story splits into five legendary survival stories, each one involving heroism of the utmost degree, each one singly an epic tale of against-all odds:

a. The ship *Endurance*'s crushing and the survival of the men on the ice floes of the Weddell Sea;

b. The harrowing journey to a jutting rock called Elephant Island in the three small lifeboats;

c. The 17-day open-boat journey of 800 miles in a 22-foot double-ended lifeboat, the *James Caird*, on the world's stormiest sea—the same waters that sank four of Sir Francis Drake's ships several centuries earlier;

d. The climb across the ice-bound mountaintops of South Georgia, which had never been attempted, the highest peak being Mount Paget (9000 feet). To get to the other side of South Georgia they had to cross two snowfields, four glaciers, and three mountain ranges—all unmapped, each one life-threatening;

e. The survival and rescue of 22 men marooned for 137 days on gale-swept Elephant Island; it took four attempts for Shackleton to snatch his men from the jaws of Antarctic winter and ice.

Could one of the sea's greatest sailors be a leadership guide and guru for teaching us a hundred years later how to sail new seas—and survive shipwrecks?

Relational Leaders

Leadership has been the buzzword of the nineties and naughts. The birthing, breeding, and building of leaders is the focus of much scholarly scrutiny and popular attention. Leaders like Shackleton who did not lead from the rear—cautious, bases-covered, consensus-building leadership—but stepped up to the plate and put their lives on the line have exceptional appeal. The long lines of people waiting to get into the "Shackleton Exhibit" as it made its way across North America attest to that.[30]

> Courage and willpower can make miracles,
> I know of no better example than what that man has accomplished.
>
> —Roald Amundsen[29]

One of the reasons Shackleton "failed" is that relationships were more important to him than achievement, colleagues more important than conquests and campaigns. Shackleton pioneered a relational-based leadership style that is only beginning to be grasped today. His ultimate claim to fame was that in all of his explorations, "he never lost a man." Unlike explorers who recklessly sacrificed lives for mission, Shackleton modulated a mission if it entailed the loss of even one life.

Extreme Experiences

Natives in today's emerging culture are extremophiles—infatuated with "extremes," whether it be "extreme sports" or extreme life forms (e.g., thermal vents in the bottom of the sea) or extreme conditions (hurricanes, tidal waves, tornadoes). Life that is lived in the most inhospitable settings has particular appeal.

There is no more extreme setting than the Antarctic—the last great wilderness, a "crystal desert" covering 10 percent of the earth's land surface and holding 90 perecent of the world's snow and ice. Whatever "most" one can think of, it applies to this 7 million square miles of frozen sea: the most hostile, most desolate, most frigid, most windy, most barren, most dry, most elevated, outermost place on planet Earth.[31] In winter the Antarctic boasts temperatures of 100 degrees below zero and winds of 200 mph. The Southern Sea is the most treacherous water on the planet, with swells of 15 feet on calm days, and 100-foot-high waves on stormy days, some of them coming in pairs and even fearsome triplets (known as "Three Sisters Waves"). It's the harshest climate on planet Earth.

The Sounds of Shackleton

This book does not intend or pretend to retell the Shackleton chronicle one more time. This macho story has already been well told by three women. The pages of Caroline Alexander's pacy, racy narrative turn themselves (*The Endurance,* 1998); the probing anatomy of Jennifer Armstrong arrests the reader with button-holing intensity (*Shipwreck at the Bottom of the World,* 1998); and the narrative flair of Kim Heacox tells the story beautifully (*Shackleton: The Antarctic Challenge,* 1999). In fact, I purposefully do *not* want to retell the well-explored journey of the *Endurance,* since each one of the five survival stories, which add up to the maritime equivalent of walking on the moon, are so mesmeric that it is hard to focus on the under-explored strategies and secrets that made the impossible possible.

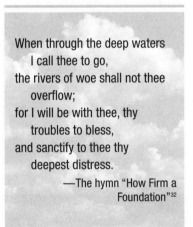

When through the deep waters
I call thee to go,
the rivers of woe shall not thee
overflow;
for I will be with thee, thy
troubles to bless,
and sanctify to thee thy
deepest distress.

—The hymn "How Firm a
Foundation"[32]

What I do hope to do in the course of this small book is to use the Shackleton saga as foil and fodder for the theory that "it's all about voice"—and to unpack what the leadership voice means for understanding sound leadership and the cultural meanings of soundful leadership.[33] If a good test of any book is the beauty of its quotations, a test of the "forget-the-vision-thing" thesis will be the beauty and merit of the Shackleton voices.

NOTES

1. William Newton Clarke, *The Christian Doctrine of God* (New York: Charles Scribner's Sons, 1909), 467.
2. As to how this quote has penetrated into various arenas, see its use in Richard Higginson, *Transforming Leadership: A Christian Approach to Management* (London: SPCK, 1996), 84. Warren Bennis's most recent book, a bellweather for a radical turn in leadership literature, argues that every leader undergoes at least one life-transforming "crucible" experience, a make-or-break event that helps a person become a leader. See Warren G. Bennis and Robert J. Thomas, *Geeks and Geezers: How Era, Values, and Defining Moments Shape Leaders* (Cambridge, MA: Harvard Business School Press, 2002), 14–18, 87–120.
3. Quoted in Higginson, *Transforming Leadership*, 26.
4. See Bob Woodward, *Bush at War* (New York: Simon & Schuster, 2002), 341.
5. At best, between 35 and 40% of "leadership qualities" are inheritable, according to one recent study cited in " Creating Leaders," in the insert "Tough at the Top: A Survey of Leadership," The Economist (25 October 4, 2003), 7.
6. Coleman Cornelius, "A 7-Year-Old's Act of Courage," *Denver Post* (11 December 2002), 1, 8A, 9A.
7. As quoted in Stewart Alsop, "Eating My Own Words: A Letter to Lou Gerstner," *Fortune* (18 February 2002), 64. www.fortune.com/fortune/investing/articles/0,15114,371925,00.html. Accessed 29 May 2003.
8. Tom Peters and Bob Waterman, *In Search of Excellence: Lessons from American's Best Run Companies* (New York: Harper & Row, 1982) and Jim Collins and Jerry Porras, *Built to Last: Successful Habits of Visionary Companies* (New York: HarperBusiness, 1994).
9. Quoted in Joshua Macht, "Jim Collins to CEOs: Lose the Charisma," *Business 2.0* (October 2001), 121. Collins says, "Charisma can be as much a liability as an asset, as the strength of your leadership personality can deter people from bringing you the brutal facts" (Jim Collins, *Good to Great: Why Some Companies Make the Leap . . . Others Don't* [New York: HarperCollins, 2001], 89). www.business2.com/articles/mag/0,1640,17013,00.html. Accessed 20 December 2002.
10. As quoted in Jerry Useem, "America's Most Admired Companies," *Fortune* (19 February 2001), 96. www.fortune.com/fortune/mostadmired/articles/0,15114,372370,00.html. Accessed 27 April 2003.

11. Collins, *Good to Great*, 17–40.
12. Ibid., 164–65.
13. Jim Collins and Jerry I. Porras, *Built to Last: Successful Habits of Visionary Companies* (New York: HarperBusiness, 1994), 34.
14. For the confusion about leadership in religious circles, see George Barna:

    - Research demonstrates the increasing importance of—and confusion regarding—leadership. Drawing on that research, we have just released a new book (*A Fish Out of Water*) and a related self-administered leadership evaluation tool (*Christian Leader Profile©*.
    - Confusion reigns! More than nine out of ten Protestant Senior Pastors claimed to be leaders—until we posed a specific definition of a leader (at which time the percentage dropped below two-thirds) or asked if they felt God had entrusted one of the leadership-related gifts to them (at which time the ratio dipped below one in four).
    - Protestant Senior Pastors are most likely to assert that they are leaders because they feel they do a good job in the areas of teaching and providing encouragement to people; in fact, they rated themselves comparatively poorly regarding leadership functions.
    - Less than 2% of Protestant Senior Pastors believe they do a below-average job of leading their congregation, which suggests that many pastors do not have an accurate view of their leadership performance.

    (Quoted in Barna Research Updates—Family Matters, "New Book and Diagnostic Resource Strive to Clear Up Widespread Confusion Regarding Leadership," 5 August 2002.) www.timlive.com/BarnaResearch/Confusion_ Regarding_Leadership.asp. Accessed 20 December 2002.
    Barna Research has developed the "Christian Leader Profile©," a self-administered inventory allowing individuals to discover objective, faith-based evaluations of their calling to leadership, the quality of their character, their strongest competencies, and aptitude for leadership. See "Clarify Your Leadership Potential and Status—Use the Christian Leader Profile," www.barna.org/cgi-bin/ clp/home.asp, or click on the Christian Leader Profile icon on Barna's home page, www.barna.org. Accessed 16 November 2003.
15. Michael Treacy, author of *Discipline of Market Leaders* as quoted in Erick Schonfeld, "$50,000 for Your Thoughts," *Business 2.0* (October 2001), 60.
16. Martin Kasindorf, "Voters Never Really grew Fond of David," *USA Today* (8 October 2003), 17A.
17. See John E. Roueche, George A. Baker III, and Robert R. Rose, *Shared Vision: Transformational Leadership in American Community Colleges* (Washington, DC: Community College Press, 1989), 19. See also Bernard M. Bass, *Stogdill's Handbook of Leadership: A Survey of Theory and Research* (New York: Free Press, 1981), 5, which states, "Leadership is one of the most observed and least understood phenomena on earth."
18. Joseph C. Rost, *Leadership for the Twenty-first Century* (New York: Praeger, 1991), 99.
19. Sir Raymond Priestley of the *Nimrod* expedition (1907–9), as quoted in Harding McGregor Dunnett, *Shackleton's Boat: The Story of the James Caird*

(Benenden, Kent: Neville & Harding, 1996), 96. Granddaughter Alexandra Shackleton attributes this quote to James Boyd Adams in her foreword to Kim Heacox, *Shackleton: The Antarctic Challenge* (Washington, DC: National Geographic Society, 1999), 6.

20. Vernon Watkins, "I, Centurion," in *The Collected Poems of Vernon Watkins* (Ipswich, Suffolk: Golgonooza: 1986), 265.

21. Dudley Farfield, "It Could Have Been Worse (Much Worse)," *Forbes FYI: The Good Life: Travel Issue Supplement* (Spring 1998), 134–42. In the case of Stanley, it was not the "Dr. Livingstone, I presume?" expedition, but the one three years later in 1874 (134).

22. As quoted in the frontispiece to Jennifer Armstrong, *Shipwreck at the Bottom of the World: The Extraordinary True Story of Shackleton and the Endurance* (New York: Crown, 1998). Another source says the original quote came from Sir Raymond Priestley, a member of the *Nimrod* expedition of 1907–9 (as cited in Dunnett, *Shackleton's Boat*, 96):

> For scientific leadership, give me Scott, for swift and efficient travel, Amundsen. But when you are in a hopeless situation, when you are seeing no way out, get down on your knees and pray for Shackleton. Incomparable in adversity, he was the miracle worker who would save your life against all the odds and long after your number was up. The greatest leader that ever came on God's earth, bar none.

23. Pray was from the 62nd Aircraft Wing at McChord Air Force Base near Tacoma. See Patrick McMahon, "Special Delivery to Bottom of World: Emergency Items Reach South Pole," *USAToday*, 12 July 1999, 3A; available on line as "Emergency Supplies Dropped at South Pole," *USAToday Cold Science, Reports on the Antarctic and Arctic*, updated 17 April 2000. www.usatoday.com/weather/antarc/aspdrop.htm. Accessed 1 September 2001. See also Thomas Hayden and Adam Rogers, "Nowhere to Go for Help" in *Newsweek* (26 July 1999), 68.

24. Psalm 107:23–25 NASB.

25. Armstrong, *Shipwreck at the Bottom of the World*, 9.

26. Caroline Alexander, *The Endurance: Shackleton's Legendary Antarctic Expedition* (New York: Alfred A. Knopf, 1998).

27. Stephanie Capparell, "Shackleton's Techniques for Surviving Antarctica Inspire Business Leaders," *Wall Street Journal*, 19 December 2000, B1.

28. From Ringo Starr, "There's a Good Life Had at Sea (Sail Away Raymond)," as quoted in www.ciudadfutura.com/poprock/ringsuns.html. Accessed 23 November 2002.

29. The first part of the tribute—"Sir Ernest Shackleton's name will for evermore be engraved with letters of fire in the history of Antarctic exploration"—serves as the frontispiece to Roland Huntford, *Shackleton* (New York: Carroll & Graf, 1985), where the full tribute is quoted on page 692.

30. The Shackleton Exhibit was developed by the American Museum of Natural History in 1999 and toured several major cities in USAmerica. The exhibit grew out of the discovery by author Caroline Alexander of numerous photographs taken by the expedition's official photographer, Frank Hurley.

31. Christopher C. Joyner, *Governing the Frozen Commons: The Antarctic Regime and Environmental Protection* (Columbia: University of South Carolina Press, 1998), 1.

32. Attributed to "K" in Rippon's *A Selection of Hymns*, 1787, as found in *The United Methodist Hymnal: Book of United Methodist Worship* (Nashville: United Methodist Publishing House, 1989), 529.

33. One of the few leadership writers to call attention to the ear as well as the eye is Harriet Rubin: "There's a lot to be said for vision and values, but what about the voice of leadership? . . . Leaders are judged even more by the music of their words than by whether they live up to them. We can't hear the music in Al Gore, so we condemn him for not speaking from the soul. George W. Bush works hard to convey a tone of seriousness, and we listen for that even more than we do for his platform. It's all music" (Harriet Rubin, "Living Dangerously," *Fast Company* [November 2000], 410–13, 412). www.fastcompany.com/magazine/40/hrubin.html. Accessed 27 May 2002.

The Power of Voice

Finding Your Personal Soundtrack

> Let us hope the 21st century seeks universality at the smallest scale, that it recognizes that the fullness of existence is contained in the tiniest of spaces.
>
> —Economist Leopold Kohr[1]

Can one person change the course of history?

More now than ever.

This may have been a question for historians in the past, but no more. Now more than ever, it is possible for individuals to have that kind of impact on the world. The only question is how, what, when, or where one person will change history. There is now no such thing as an unhistoric act. Every person decides whether their footprints will last beyond a lifetime or sink in the sands of time.

THE POWER OF ONE

Visionary leaders see possibilities. Called-forth leaders actually turn those possibilities into realities. Hebrew history scholar George Adam Smith makes this compelling analogy from the natural environment of the Middle East:

> Great men are not the whole of life, but they are the condition of all the rest; if it were not for the big men, the little ones could scarcely live.... In the East ... where the desert touches a river-valley or oasis, the sand is in a continual state

of drift from the wind ... which is the real cause of the bar-renness of such portions of the desert at least as abut upon the fertile land. ... But set down a rock on the sand, and see the difference its presence makes. After a few showers, to the leeward side of this some blades will spring up; if you have patience, you will see in time a garden. How has the boulder produced this? Simply by arresting the drift.

Now this is exactly how great men benefit human life. A great man serves his generation, serves the whole race, by arresting the drift.[2]

When you think of yourself as a leader, is this how you think? Do you imagine yourself changing the course of history? For too long the church has abdicated that role to others, but it is my conviction that this is the kind of leader we are called to become. Everyone has the responsibility and right to write their own history. Leaders have the responsibility and right to write our common future.

What makes possible this phenomenon whereby the more global the economy, the more pivotal and powerful the indi-vidual, and the more every person can be called forth to become a soundful leader? The answer lies in the energy of the split atom, the genetic secrets of the Book of Life, the invisi-ble connectivity of the Web. When these are added to our means, the Power of One has never been greater. One of the greatest tragedies of history is that so many times the Power of One will *not* make history: the child dying of malaria in Zim-babwe; the teenager whose life is snuffed out by landmines or smart-bombs; the middle-aged corporate climber driving to work in a spacious Mercedes to live his life in an empty, cramped cubicle; the housewife who plays the part everyone wants her to play.

We can no longer hide behind the excuse that only the gifted or the privileged can change the course of history. We live in a time when we are not bound by position or geography or circumstance. If you hear the summons—if you know your cause—nothing can stand in the way.

A DISTINGUISHING PERSONAL SOUNDTRACK

In my high school orchestra I played the bassoon. But in the marching band I played the cymbals or the big bass drum. You couldn't march with a bassoon.

Ever notice how the drum set is the only instrument we all think we can play without lessons? If there's a drum, we're drawn to it. A cymbal attracts pinging. A clarinet or bassoon is foreboding and off-putting. A guitar is hard to pick up. But not a drum. We immediately begin rat-a-tat-tatting on the snare drum. Everybody thinks they're Ringo Starr or Phil Collins.

Each of us has our own personal rhythm. We all march to our own beat, a beat we play out on the drums and cymbals of our lives.

What is the beat, the cadence, the cycle in your life? What is the soundtrack that fits your personal rhythm and voice?

To leverage the Power of One, every person needs to find their own Power of Voice—a personal soundtrack that rings true, with a voice-activated aura that can become larger than life. As we read in the Old Testament the account of Samuel's becoming a great leader, it is important to remember that his mentor's eyes were weak. Yet Eli knew a summons when he heard it, and he helped Samuel answer the call. Only then did Samuel find his voice.

Older treatises on leadership that highlighted "charisma" were on the right track but had the wrong concept. It's not the power of the "charisma" that makes the difference. It's the power of voice. It's the development of an inner ear trained and to trust and try the inner voice.[3]

My favorite 20th-century poet, Denise Levertov, says,

> I believe fervently that the poet's first obligation is to his own voice—to find it and use it. And one's "voice" does not speak

only in the often slip-shod imprecise vocabulary with which one buys the groceries but with all the resources of one's life whatever they may be, no matter whether they are "American" or of other cultures, so long as they are truly one's own and not faked.[5]

Everyone is voice-activated because music is everyone's first language.[6] All art, including and especially the art of acoustic leadership, aspires toward the primal and primeval mode of music. In fact, William Benzon talks about making music ("musicking") as a social phenomenon that actually creates a physical coupling between otherwise separate neurosystems. He suggests using "music" as a verb.[7] Some have even suggested that the Berlin Wall and the Cold War were musicked out of existence.

All leaders music themselves and others in voice-finding and voice-making. The art of musicking is finding your own voice and learning how to control the voice you project. Leaders are pied pipers. Humans follow the music. If the choice is between a tone-deaf visionary and a dullard with a voice, guess who wins?

> There are silences harder to take back than words.
> —Poet James Richardson[8]

But while every leader's voice is unrepeatable, it is not irreplaceable. There were arguably only two leaders in USAmerican history whose voice was irreplaceable: Abraham Lincoln and Martin Luther King Jr.

You don't lead. No one does. You only exercise leadership. Leadership is not a position or office or appointment. Leadership is a function of voice, a process of discourse and discovery.[9] The worst thing you can do is to take a leadership position. The best thing you can do is to create a leadership experience through a distinguishing personal soundtrack.

The church has it all wrong. It is trying to train leaders. Instead, it ought to train everyone to listen and to develop their own soundtrack. Only when you find your voice will you harness the God-given power to truly lead.

In spring 2003 the Securities and Exchange Commission reached a $22 million settlement with former officials of Xerox Corporation. The SEC found that the executives had illegally inflated revenues by billions of dollars in the late 1990s and had set an improper "tone at the top" of their company, which enabled underlings to play tricks on regulators and shareholders. "It is crucial," the SEC said in its ruling, "that public companies have a tone at the top that reflects corporate ethics and good corporate governance."[11]

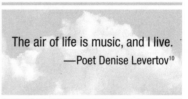

The air of life is music, and I live. ·
—Poet Denise Levertov[10]

There are four keynotes, four "tones at the top" of a distinguishing personal soundtrack.

Keynote #1: Telling the Truth

The essence of a voice's integrity is fidelity to the truth. Truth is the dominant seventh without which there are no harmonies.

But what truth? The truth about yourself? The truth about others? The truth about life? The truth about reality?

A historian's job is to tell the truth about the past. A consultant's job is to tell the truth about the present. A psychiatrist's job is to help you tell the truth about who you are. A theologian's job is to tell the truth about God. A leader's job is to rise to the occasion, to imagine the best possible future, and to tell the truth about how to get there. A leader's voice rings the bell of the future.

Leadership integrity is arts and crafts: the art of musicking the best possible future, and the crafting of strategies to get there. Soundful leaders lead for tomorrow, not for the quarterly financial statement. Soulful leaders find moments of crisis making the voice of prophecy even more commanding and comforting.

This doesn't mean that a leader's words and actions have parted company, but rather that an authentic personal soundtrack absorbs the musical language of a people's fears, uncertainties, hopes, dreams. It turns mayhem into marches, desperation into determination, resignation into resistance, facts into fantasy. The voice of a leader communicates truth beyond words, truth that sometimes goes beyond even the comprehension of leaders themselves. Leaders are those for whom voice—even more than words—is a way of life.

Is it surprising that King David spent so much of his time making music? Or that one of the great treatises on leadership—the Old Testament book of Psalms—is a collection of music?

The notion that the true poet must first be a true poem, as Puritan poet John Milton insisted, fails to account for history.[12] Some of our greatest poets and musicians lived lives of failed poems and ghastly music. In addition, every one of us falls from grace. Not one of us can claim total consistency between who we appear to be and who we are. No one gets through life without being capsized by a thousand compromises. A good leader is different from a leader who looks good.

The fundamental harmony between what is said and what is led lies in the realm of participation, not performance. Voice-activated leadership is a participation art—a leader must participate in what's being led and must call others into the partnership of forging a future. Leadership is high-risk, action-oriented, and not afraid of modeling, mentoring, and musicking the kind of human beings—in spite of all the attendant stumbles and flaws—that we are asking others to emulate. A leader steps up to the plate, takes a swing, and hands the bat on. A leader sounds a call but summons participation. In the future, all leadership will be less "informative" and more "formative."

Keynote #2: Promoting Social Justice and Spiritual Vibrancy

Distinguishing personal soundtracks should make the world more socially just and more spiritually vibrant. When a soundtrack is in place, leaders make decisions, not according to what's in their best *interest*, but according to what's in their best *values*. When he received the Mondello Prize for his book *Occhiacci di Legno* (1998), Carlo Ginzburg declared, "Today the word 'truth' must carry a built-in set of inverted commas."[14]

Hence the crisis of leadership that almost daily occupies the front page of the *Wall Street Journal*. Leaders build futures around *shared* values—values

> The greatest man is he who chooses right with invincible resolution, who resists the sorest temptation from within and without, who bears the heaviest burdens cheerfully; who is calmest in storms, and most fearless under menaces and frowns; whose reliance on truth, on virtue, on God, is most unfaltering.
>
> —19th-century cleric William Ellery Channing[13]

that don't change—while helping people come to terms with change.

However, values without virtues are like air-kisses without skin-landings. Values need to be hitched to virtues. To reach for "value creation" without ever hitting a moral chord is to have drained all virtue from the word *value*. In today's bottom-line living, too many decisions bottom-out at self-interest. We sort of expect that to happen in the business world, but it also happens in the church. When one's bottom-line values are supported by virtues, "survivors" are trumped by servers. When true biblical values rule, values overrule self-interest.

Of course, our ideals change as our perceptions change. But the soundtrack of industrial-strength ideals, a moral system of culture's highest and wisest virtues (especially the three transcendentals of being—beauty, truth, goodness), remains the same. One is willing to live and die by these ideals, which originate with God.

In December 1954 Winston Churchill turned eighty. President Dwight D. Eisenhower offered a list of the qualities great leaders should possess. "Vision, integrity, courage, understanding, the power of articulation . . . and profundity of character" were the marks of leadership, and Eisenhower believed that Churchill "came nearest to fulfilling the requirements of greatness in any individual that I have met in my lifetime."[15]

What matters is not the products you make, but the virtues that make you. If leadership does not attach the virtue factor to values, then a well-stocked gallery of 20th-century monsters come out as some of the greatest leaders who ever lived. Stalin, Hitler, Pol Pot, and Milosevic wielded immense power. But they did not lead.

Hitler had a firm set of values—without virtues. He understood the German people's needs—and kneaded them like so much silly putty through the sheer power of his voice. But Hitler did not lead the German people.[16] It is one thing to exalt a people; it is quite another thing to ennoble them. The voice of a true leader elevates a people.

J. R. Ewing was the fictional oil executive whom television viewers used to love to hate. J.R. said on one episode of *Dallas* (1978–91), "Once you give up your ethics, the rest is a piece of cake."

It is not enough to point to our biblically informed values and claim the moral high ground. Ethics may be an elective in seminary, but it is a required course in the real world of leading. Once you give up your ethics, life *isn't* a piece of cake. It's a disaster.

Rich soundtracks issue in acts that inch our world toward greater responsibility and humility. The modern architect Le Corbusier once called medieval cathedrals "acts of optimism." Whenever a door slams shut, a leader breathes the fresh air of an opening window—and embarks on another cathedral-like display of ambition and hope. Before reaching that final anchorage in the sky, leaders build "acts of optimism": acts of imagination envisioning new realities that prove seaworthy for whatever waters in which they find themselves.

A leader is someone willing to build an ark in the dark. Noah listened to a call that others heard as foolishness. Too much of how we lead in the church is based on trying to please everyone but the One who matters. Every ethical shortcut we take, no matter how small, dampens the music of our leadership.

Keynote #3: Generating Original Sounds

Third, personal soundtracks should give off an original sound. The word *original* carries two senses. The first is the originality of voice-hardware that comes from recombining old sounds into fresh forms. Find me a "new idea," and I'll find you an existing idea genetically engineered, an "already said" in an antique package. True originality is homecoming. Argentinian writer Jorge Luis Borges (1899–1986) summed up the phenomenon of the "already said" with the following aphorism: "To speak is to commit tautologies."[17]

Sir Isaac Newton and Gottfried Wilhelm Leibniz came up with the calculator during the same ten-day period. Newton spent the rest of his life trying to prove that Leibniz had ripped him off, thereby preventing him from doing some potentially great work. Robert Noyce and Jack Kilby invented the microchip independently of each other. They both used silicon. Both their inventions involved transistors. How can this be? They both drew on the same intellectual heritage and came up with the same thing.

Scientists and musicians aren't alone in studding their creations with quotations from other people's works. (Listen to the finale of Dmitri Shostakovich's *Fifteenth Symphony*). Charles Dickens filched phrases, images, and fragments of speech far in advance of incorporating them into his manuscript. "Baudelaire was not a shopper," observes a perceptive Baudelaire scholar; "he was a burglar, stealing ideas and erasing their original contexts."[18] Baudelaire even tried to steal the only thing original about the human species according to Christianity, the idea of "original sin," placing it in an entirely new setting. Lytton Strachey was larcenous with literary sources, never more so than in his most original book, *The Eminent Victorians* (1918).[19] Philosopher Henry James was a kleptomaniac with words, notorious for his "appropriations."[20] Karl Marx lifted other people's expressions, although not on the scale of Oscar Wilde, James Whistler, or Edith Wharton.[21] Some Dylanologist is always turning up borrowings from books or films, with portions of *Love and Theft* (2003) lifted from a yakuza novel. It was T. S. Eliot who said, "Immature poets imitate, mature poets steal"[22]—not Lionel Trilling, as many collections have it. What Trilling actually said was "Immature artists imitate, mature artists steal,"[23] proving Eliot's point.[24]

"The trouble with ancients," Mark Twain quipped, "is that they stole all our ideas." Only Adam and Eve can claim words without quotes, ideas without echoes. To be human is to wear the battle honors of the losing fight against the ultimate human-"ism": plagiarism.[25]

The "genius" of Christianity, according to sociologist David Martin, is its creativity in using "mosaics of phrases, metaphors and images." The earliest Christians boldly reassembled and then dramatically enlarged fragments of hope and shafts of insight originally found in the Hebrew scriptures. "Our greatest hymns (and sermons too) are also mosaics of quotation. Prayers, hymns, sermons are echo chambers of quotation concerning what is known by heart and inscribed there." If the Christian life is a quotation of Jesus, then "loss of faith is closely linked to loss of the quotations we have by heart."[26]

The striking thing about Jesus is not his originality. It's his derivativeness. Jesus professes only to be doing whatever his Father tells him to. That's why he rebels against his family—not to go off on his own path, but to follow his Father's will and path, and bring his family with him.

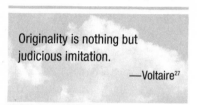

Originality is nothing but judicious imitation.

—Voltaire[27]

The second sense of the word *original* is the originality of voice-software that comes from deep within and follows a path peculiar to itself. It is this sense of originality that caused Goethe to despise the word *composed* for Mozart's opera *Don Giovanni* (1787).

> How can one say Mozart "composed" *Don Giovanni*, as if it were a piece of cake made of eggs, flour, and sugar stirred together! It is a spiritual creation, the details like the whole pervaded by a single spirit and outpouring ... not concocted from this and that, but obeying the daemonic commands of genius.[28]

Inside each of us is a yearning to follow "the commands of genius." The only question is whether we will listen regardless of where that voice takes us. The fresh wine of inner genius will always burst the wineskins of custom and comfort, yet leadership in the church so often yields to safety. Jesus was anything but safe. If history has shown anything, it is that no voice is too vanguard, too ingenious, too maverick for leadership.

Keynote #4: Sounding from Experience

Fourth, a distinguishing soundtrack is one that sounds from a well-stocked soul, a well-furnished mind, a well-appointed being. Voice-activated leaders have experienced in their own lives the world-transforming powers of art, poetry, literature, and other world-class products of the human imagination. If our faith has no room for the imagination, it is not true faith at all. We can no longer afford one-dimensional leadership.

A distinguishing soundtrack can distinguish the merely pretty from the truly beautiful. A leader is someone who has kept faith with the finest spirits of the culture into which one is born without losing "the common touch."

In the passage through life, our voice changes. The change comes by time, by events, by interventions. By things we read, things we see, things we *hear*. We learn and grow, and our voice changes. If it's not changing, we're not listening. Of course, there are changes in situation, and there are changes in state. The former is what we normally call "change"; the latter is really "transition" (as happens during puberty). The key to leadership is knowing the difference between "change" and "transition."

YOUR OWN HEART SONG

When super-string physicists tell us that we are a "vibrating loop of energy," they are really telling us that you and I are at base *sound*—the human organization of dancing energy. Sound is a function of vibrations, which give off frequencies. We *hear* something because we pick up its vibrations.

Each of us is a song. When God created you, God created you to be an unrepeatable, irreplaceable *song*, the likes of which will never be again. We are the "unheard melodies" John Keats talked about in little-known lines from his well-known poem "Ode on a Grecian Urn."

> Heard melodies are sweet, but those unheard
> Are sweeter; therefore, ye soft pipes, play on;
> Not to the sensual ear, but, more endear'd,
> Pipe to the spirit ditties of no tone.[29]

You don't have an atom in your body that isn't singing a song. Your genes, your ganglia, your liver, your lipids—every one of your trillions of cells vibrates. Do you see brainwaves? Do you see vibrations?[30]

My favorite e. e. cummings poem would replace all our modern "thou shalt nots" with one positive commandment: "you shall above all things be glad and young." It ends by zinging our Enlightenment obsession with critique and disdain for celebration:

> I'd rather learn from one bird how to sing
> than teach ten thousand stars how not to dance.[31]

Learn to love the sound of your own voice, and then learn to use your voice to bring out others' voices. Voice-activated leadership is giving people a song to sing.

A woman appearing before the Texas state legislature, speaking on behalf of state funding for the arts, made this statement: "Give me shoes and they last for a year. Give me groceries and they last for a week. Give me a song and it lasts for a lifetime."

> In reason's ear they all rejoice,
> and utter forth a glorious voice;
> Forever singing, as they shine,
> "The hand that made us is divine."
>
> —Joseph Addison (1672–1719)[32]

Welsh-English physician Ernest Lloyd used to lecture his students in the mysteries of the heart. He would crescendo the heart's wonders until he dropped to a whisper: "Have you ever heard a mitral murmur, boys, have you? It's like the wind rustling through the golden corn. You think I'm being poetic? Why, when you listen with your stethoscope to the old heart, boys, you are listening to a kind of poetry."[33]

That old Welsh doctor didn't know how right he was. Scientists have been debating what the next advance in biometrics beyond "fingerprints" would be. Some argue for face recognition;

others, hand geometry and signature verification. The most popular candidate, however, has been "soundprints"—human "sound pictures" (sonograms) made by a computer breaking your voice down into intervals a thousandth of a second long, each interval containing thousands of frequencies of sound, which the computer lays out on a graph that generates your unique "soundprint."

Researchers at Beth Israel Hospital in Boston have taken "soundprints" one step farther. They have discovered that every heartbeat gives off certain frequencies that are totally unique. These frequencies create a pattern of sound that is uniquely yours, and it goes by the name of "Heart Songs." One of these researchers has hired a composer to put his own "heart song" into symphonic form.[34]

> The earth keeps some vibration going
> There in your heart, and that is you.
> —Poet Edgar Lee Masters[35]

In May 1998 Mikhail Baryshnikov gave an unprecedented solo ballet performance. "An Evening of Music and Dance" featured "HeartBeat: mb," an improvisation to his own heart song amplified through a wireless device affixed to his shirtless chest.[36]

Each of us must learn to sing *by heart* our personal song.

SHACKLETON MODULATIONS: | **Optimism • Integrity • Idealism • Endurance**

When Ernest Shackleton was asked what he looked for in his men, he told *Pearson's* magazine the qualities essential in an Antarctic explorer: "First, optimism; second, patience; third, physical endurance; fourth, idealism; fifth and last, courage."[37] Maybe that's why Captain Robert Scott chose the 28-year-old merchant seaman Ernest Shackleton for his National Antarctic Expedition aboard the *Discovery*.

Sir Ernest Shackleton found his voice and filled it on his third expedition to the Antarctic beginning aboard the *Endurance*. Shackleton's signature voice was one of optimism, integrity, idealism, endurance, and a love of the sea.

Optimism

"Optimism is true moral courage," Shackleton said, a conviction he practiced daily as he whiled away his hours, always displaying his own towering "moral courage" in the midst of his crew.

On January 19, 1915, the Antarctic ice held the *Endurance* in its frozen teeth. Shackleton and his 27-man crew had sailed nearly halfway round the world and had maneuvered through 1000 miles of pack ice. But they were stopped in the ice, unable to see open water anywhere. They were less than 100 miles from the Antarctic continent, but that's as close as they would get. At any minute they were at risk of slipping off the bottom edge of the earth.

The seamen drifted for over nine months, through an Antarctic winter, on a ship frozen into the ice. In those days no communication was possible between the explorers and the world they had left behind. When summer was approaching and they had drifted far enough northward that they hoped the ship would soon be freed from nature's frozen grip and grave, the shifting ice instead crushed the ship into so much firewood, stranding Shackleton and his devastated crew *on* the ice.

With supplies from the ship and three lifeboats atop the ice, they drifted for almost six more months amidst the polar ice pack on an ice floe that gradually diminished from a half-mile across to the size of a couple of tennis courts. From the time *Endurance* was trapped by the ice until the crew launched the lifeboats, they had traveled 600 miles and survived over 15 months in the Antarctic. On the day the ice floe broke up with them on it, Shackleton calmly wrote in his diary:

> Our little boats may be compelled any day now to sail unsheltered over the open sea with a thousand leagues of ocean separating them from the land to the north and east. It seems vital that we should land on Clarence Island or its neighbor, Elephant Island.[38]

If they missed these islands, all hope would be lost. They weren't in an area where rescuers might look for them. Elephant Island was an uninhabited rock only 20 miles long, and it was over 100 miles away in the Southern Ocean, the most storm-swept waters in the world. The Southern Ocean routinely sees 60-knot winds and 70-foot waves. The water temperature is seldom higher than 33 degrees, a fact that fastens to the mind and body when someone sailing these seas never gets dry.

Even when things looked bleakest, Shackleton always managed to inspire hope that kept his men going. "We were full of hope and optimism," the second-in-command New Zealander named Frank Worsley remembered, "feelings that Shackleton always fostered."[39]

On April 8, Shackleton, fondly known as "The Boss," gave the order: "Launch the boats."

The lead boat was the largest: the 22-foot *James Caird*. In it rode Shackleton and 11 of his men.[40] Worsley captained the second boat, the *Dudley Docker*, transporting eight more men.[41] In the rear was the smallest boat, the *Stancomb Wills*, carrying the last seven crew members.[42]

From Worsley's journal we learn what happened when the three boats tried to make a run for it through the bergs and floes:

> So far this boat escape had been a "rake's progress." We had rowed. We had sailed. Shackleton and I had taken turns at towing the smallest boat. We had been hindered by pack ice, head winds, currents and heavy swells. We had hauled up on the ice and escaped again. Now, after three days of toil and exposure,

without sleep, we were forty miles further from Elephant Island. In spite of all, the men, inspired by Shackleton were magnificent. Their courage and humour came to the front when most needed.[43]

Shackleton's voice of optimism kept everyone going, even when all seemed lost.

Integrity

The integrity of Shackleton's voice was not his truth-telling about the bleakness of

> All I ask is a tall ship and a star to steer her by.
> —Poet laureate John Masefield[44]

their situation, or his own suspicions about their survival. Shackleton voiced the truth about what it would take for them to have a future. Given the blasts of reality that assaulted the expedition daily, it was not always an easy tune to sing, or to get others to sing along with him.

Shackleton's words and actions rang true in his willingness to do anything he asked his men to do. He led by participation. The Boss didn't "crack the whip from behind," but inspired the crew from up front. Rather than give orders that he expected others to carry out, he himself risked his own life and worked in front of his men doing what he asked of them. Known for having the courage "to do the job he was most afraid of," Shackleton taught his men while teaching himself to face and out-face fear. One of the crew, Third Officer Alfred Cheetham, later bragged to some ladies about his captain. "The Boss," he said,

> Aye, he's a fine leader, he is. . . . He don't run you into any danger if he can help it; but, by gum! If there's danger, he goes first.[45]

If probity is integrity taken to the next level—integrity that has been tested and found true, being who you say you are even when it costs you something—then Shackleton's probity of voice ran deep. He proved this when he willingly abandoned his goal of crossing the Antarctic for the sake of a greater ideal: preserving the lives of his men. Some things are more important than success and honors, such as the relationships of friends and family.

Shackleton never sidelined honesty, empathy, guilt, or a sense of fairness. Trust, integrity, and fairness matter. And they matter to the bottom line. The Boss never played fast and loose with the lives of his men.

Idealism

Sir Ernest Shackleton did more than pay his respect to truth. His voice resounded the ideals of a "family man." A "family man" who found comfort and fulfillment on the "home front," however, meant something different then than it does today. His heritage as an Englishman and a Christian was for him what today we mean by "family" and "home." God, Country, and Home were life's largest ideals.

Shackleton could never imagine identifying himself any other way than as a Christian. He wasn't a freethinker. He wasn't an agnostic. His faith was steeped in Anglican tea. He was a straight-lipped, straight-down-the-middle "Christian"— bloody red and true blue—with no mystical mishmash.

A sense of place, and loyalty to it, were intense within Shackleton. It is hard for us, living in a placeless world, to understand the pain and humiliation that came to an Englishman when Norwegian Roald Amundsen arrived at the South Pole before the Englishman Scott. Shackleton needed to achieve something for England. If they couldn't get the Pole, they would get the first transcontinental crossing of the Antarctic by way of the South Pole—a trip of 1,800 miles.

The irony of the *Endurance* steaming down the River Thames toward the Atlantic on the very day Britain entered World War I did not go unnoticed. Without question or second thoughts, Shackleton wired the Admiralty and placed his crew and ship at the disposal of the Royal Navy. Only when they received a decision from Winston Churchill, the First Lord of the Admiralty at the time, did they continue their voyage south. The one-word telegram read: "PROCEED."[47] Even then they continued to be torn and "tortured," feeling not only the pull of duty to Country to the north, but also the pull of honor for Country to the south.

The last idealistic feature of Shackleton's voice was his love of poetry, music, and the arts. He read poetry, wrote poetry, and memorized large chunks of popular poets, especially Browning, Kipling, and Tennyson. His mind was well furnished in the arts and sciences, and he incorporated three scientists into his crew. It is hard to imagine a ship as a mecca for artistic patronage and production, but this is exactly how Shackleton envisioned the *Endurance*. He hired as an expedition photographer the celebrated Australian Frank Hurley. Shackleton was savvy to the commercial value of a photographic record of his voyage. He had even raised money based on selling the film and photo rights at the end of his trip. And he kept for himself the publishing rights to the diaries of all the crewmen. He designed the entire voyage as a profit-making venture.

One might consider Shackleton's voyage the first postmodern expedition. More important than the discoveries of specimens themselves were the stories of the trip: the photos, diaries, and memories that had to be preserved at all costs.

Endurance

The vessel Shackleton purchased for his expedition, originally christened *Polaris*, was designed for the ice, sporting a four-foot-thick wooden hull. Shackleton did more than honor his family motto (*Fortitudine Vincimus*, or "By Endurance We Conquer") in renaming the ship *Endurance*.[48] He lived by and was haunted by these words. He tested these words every day of his life.

Although The Boss could write in his diary, "Patience. Patience. Patience,"[49] the word that probably best conveys what he meant is "endurance." Patience is a passive, waiting word. Endurance is an active, working word that suggests the opposite of "hang in there"—which is, after all, a horrible way to go through life, neck in noose, feet dangling in midair. When Shackleton was being most "patient," he did everything *but* "hang loose." He ran, he walked, he pulled, he pushed, he studied, he listened. He never "hung."

Shackleton's mighty voice of endurance kept him and the crew going when it would have been easy to dwell on their misfortune and mope about aimlessly. On board the ship, and later stranded on the ice, Shackleton established rituals (called "routines" or "drills") that brought a certain litany and rhythm to life: out of that rhythm, or "groove," came confidence and security to his men.

Shackleton showed the persistence of a child who, once his mind is set on something, like a dog with a bone, won't give it up. In one of the strangest but strongest commencement speeches ever given, the same man who gave Shackleton the green light to "proceed" told the graduates of Harrow School on October 29, 1941, never to hang their harp on the willow. The great lesson in Winston Churchill's commencement speech was the following:

> Never give in, never give in, *never, never, never*—
> in nothing, great or small, large or petty—never give in,
> except to convictions of honor and good sense.
> Never give in.[50]

Or, in the words of a Confederate soldier in the USCivil War, oft quoted by politicians: "Brigades, how long are we gonna fight? Till hell freezes over! And then we're gonna fight on the ice!"[51]

NOTES

1. One of the last interviews with Leopold Kohr (1909–94) was given to Marilyn Berlin Snell, who quotes this toast that Leopold made at the end of their conversation. See her "Leopold Kohr, Visionary Economist 1901-1994," *Utne Reader* (September-October 1994), 44.

2. George Adam Smith, commenting on Isaiah 32:3, as quoted in his *The Book of Isaiah*, new and rev. ed. (Garden City, NY: Doubleday/Doran, 1928), 1:257–58.

3. Warren G. Bennis and Robert J. Thomas propose that every leader needs four essential qualities to stay a leader: "adaptive capacity" (ability to survive setbacks and learn from mistakes); common vision and shared meaning; integrity; and a distinctive voice. See Warren G. Bennis and Robert J. Thomas, *Geeks and Geezers: How Era, Values, and Defining Moments Shape Leaders* (Cambridge: Harvard Business School, 2003).

5. As quoted in Valerie Trueblood, "A Fellow Feeling," *The American Poetry Review*, 28 (November-December 1999), 31-32.

6. "The first sound that every human hears is the sound of the mother's heartbeat in the dark lake water of the womb. This is the reason for our ancient resonance with the drum as a musical instrument" (John O'Donohue, Anam, *Cara: A Book of Celtic Wisdom* [New York: Cliff Street Books, 70]).

7. Benzon gives credit to Christopher Small for coining the word. See William L. Benzon, *Beethoven's Anvil: Music in Mind and Culture* (New York: Basic Books, 2001), 1.

8. James Richardson, *Vectors: Aphorisms and Ten-Second Essays* (Keene, NY: Ausable Press, 2001), 71.

9. Thanks to Kirk Hadaway for this insight.

10. The last line of Denise Levertov, "The Air of Life," in her *The Double Image* (London: Cresset Press, 1946), 41.

11. *Washington Post* (6 June 2003).

12. Milton wrote, "He who would not be frustrate of his hope to write well hereafter in laudable things ought himself to bee a true Poem" ("An Apology against a Pamphlet Call'd A Modest Confutation of the Animadversions upon the Remonstrant against Smectymnuus," in *Complete Poetry and Seleced Prose of John Milton* (New York: Modern Library, n.d.), 564.).

13. William Ellery Channing, "Self-Culture: An Address Introductory to the Franklin Lectures, Delivered at Boston, September 1838," in *The Works of William E. Channing* (Boston: American Unitarian Association, 1901), 13. Also attributed to Stoic philosopher Anneaus Seneca (4 BC–65 AD).

14. Luigi Meneghello, "Behold the Strange," *TLS: Times Literary Supplement* (6 June 1999), 26.

15. Quoted by Warren F. Kimball in "The Liberation of the Summit," *TLS: Times Literary Supplement* (27 December 2002), 6.

16. This is the point of Ronald A. Heifetz, *Leadership without Easy Answers* (Cambridge, MA: Belknap Press of Harvard University Press, 1994), 65–66. He quotes Adolf Hitler: "That is the mightiest mission of our Movement, namely, to give the searching and bewildered masses a new, firm belief, a belief which will not abandon them in these days of chaos, which they will

swear and abide by, so that at least somewhere they will again find a place where their hearts can be at rest."

17. Jorge Luis Borges, *The Library of Babel*, trans. Andrew Hurley (Boston: David R. Godine, 2000), 35.

18. Graham Robb, "Flower-Pot Philosopher," review of Bernard Howells, *Baudelaire*, TLS: *Times Literary Supplement* (24 January 1997), 25.

19. John Sutherland, "Strachey, Gentleman Burglar," TLS: *Times Literary Supplement* (5 September 2003), 13.

20. See Adeline R. Tintner, *The Book World of Henry James: Appropriating the Classics* (Ann Arbor, MI: UMI Research Press, 1987); Tintner, *The Pop World of Henry James: From Fairy Tales to Science Fiction* (Ann Arbor, MI: UMI Research Press, 1987); and Tintner, *Henry James and the Lust of the Eyes: Thirteen Artists in His Work* (Baton Rouge: Louisiana State University Press, 1993). For other authors who have appropriated James, see Adeline R. Tintner, *Henry James' Legacy: The Afterlife of His Figure and Fiction* (Baton Rouge: Louisiana State University Press, 1998).

21. Adeline R. Tintner's book *Edith Wharton in Context: Essays on Intertextuality* (Tuscaloosa: University of Alabama Press, 1999) shows how Wharton drew from her contemporaries for most of her ideas as well as images and phrases.

22. T. S. Eliot, "Philip Massinger," in *The Sacred Wood: Essays on Poetry and Criticism*, 6th ed. (1920; reprint, London: Methuen, 1948), 125.

23. Lionel Trilling, as quoted in Robert Benton and Gloria Steinem, "The Student Prince ... Five Rules for Ready Accession," *Esquire* (September 1962), 85.

24. T. S. Eliot's line "Time present and time past are both perhaps present in time future" is borrowed from Augustine's *Confessions*. The opening words of Eliot's "Journey of the Magi" are stolen from a seventeenth-century sermon by Lancelot Andrewes—"a cold coming they had of it ... just the worst time of the year ... the ways deep, the weather sharp ... the very dead of winter" (as noted by P. J. Kavanagh, "Bywords," TLS: *Times Literary Supplement* [7 January 2000], 14).

25. William Jesse in *Parochialia* (1785) laments the practice of reading others' sermons: "I conceive there are many clergymen who would compose their own sermons, if they knew how to do it" (107). For more lenient views on not having to say, "As ... has said," with a focus on being faithful more than original, see William H. Willimon, "Borrowed Thoughts on Sermonic Borrowing," *Christian Ministry* 28 (January-February 1997): 14–16. In the same issue see Laurie Tiberi, "Borrowing Is OK—Lying Is Not" (17–18).

26. David Martin, *Christian Language in the Secular City* (Burlington, VT: Ashgate Publishing, 2002), 27, 33, 29.n1.

27. As quoted in Jonathon Green, *The Cynic's Lexicon* (New York: St. Martin's Press, 1984), 199.

28. As quoted by Andrew Porter in "Composed Characters," TLS: *Times Literary Supplement* (15 June 2001), 22.

29. John Keats, "Ode on a Grecian Urn," in his *Poems* (London: George Bell, 1971), 236. With thanks to Marshall Brown's "Unheard Melodies: The Force of Form" in his *Turning Points: Essays in the History of Cultural Expressions* (Stanford, CA: Stanford University Press, 1997), 242.

30. Joachim-Ernst Berendt, *Nada Brahma: The World Is Sound: Music and the Landscape of Consciousness* (Rochester, VT: Destiny Books, 1987), 40.
31. E. E. Cummings: *Complete Poems 1904-1962*, ed. George J. Firmage (New York: Liveright, 1991), 484.
32. Joseph Addison, "The Spacious Firmament on High," in *At Worship: A Hymnal for Young Churchmen* (New York: Harper, 1951), 12.
33. Dannie Abse, *Intermittent Journals* (Bridgend, Wales: Seren, 1994), 131.
34. The composer, who writes under the penname of Zack Davids, worked with his cardiologist father, Dr. Ary Goldberger. See Linda Mahdesian, "Musical Success Comes in a Heartbeat for Undergraduate," *George Street Journal* 20, no. 14. www.brown.edu/Administration/George_Street_Journal/v20/v20n14/heartsong.html. Accessed 26 April 2003.
35. Edgar Lee Masters, "Fiddler Jones," in his *Spoon River Anthology*, ed. with and introd. by John E. Hallwas (Urbana: University of Illinois Press, 1992), 147.
36. "Janney and Baryshnikov Create Electrocardio-choriography," *TechTalk* (13 May 1998). http://web.mit.edu/newsoffice/tt/1998/may13/artheart.html. Accessed 26 April 2003.
37. Ernest Shackleton, "The Making of an Explorer," *Pearson's* 38 (August 1914), 138.
38. Ernest Shackleton, *South: The Story of Shackleton's 1914–1917 Expedition* (London: Heinemann, 1970), 53.
39. Quoted in Jennifer Armstrong, *Shipwreck at the Bottom of the World: The Extraordinary True Story of Shackleton and the Endurance* (New York: Crown, 1998), 81.
40. As identified in Alfred Lansing, *Endurance: Shackleton's Incredible Voyage* (New York: McGraw-Hill, 1959), viii: Frank Wild (second-in-command), Dr. James A. McIlroy (surgeon), James M. Wordie (geologist), Leonard D. A. Hussey (meteorologist), Reginald W. James (physicist), Robert S. Clark (biologist), Frank Hurley (official photographer), Timothy McCarthy (seaman), Charles Green (cook), Harry McNeish (carpenter), and John Vincent (seaman).
41. Ibid. As identified by Lansing: Frank Worsley (captain), Lionel Greenstreet (first officer), Alfred Cheetham (third officer), A. J. Kerr (second engineer), Dr. Alexander H. Macklin (surgeon), George E. Marston (official artist), Thomas H. Orde-Lees (motor expert/storekeeper), Thomas McLeod (seaman), and Ernest Holness (fireman).
42. Ibid. As identified by Lansing: Thomas Crean (second officer), Hubert T. Hudson (navigator), Louis Rickinson (first officer), Walter How (seaman), William Bakewell (seaman), William Stevenson (fireman), and stowaway Perce Blackborrow (later steward).
43. F. A. Worsley, *Shackleton's Boat Journey* (New York: W. W. Norton, 1977), 50–51.
44. John Masefield, "Sea-Fever," in his *Salt-Water Ballads*, reprinted in his *Poems* (New York: Macmillan, 1958), 20.
45. Armstrong, *Shipwreck at the Bottom of the World*, 9.
47. Armstrong, *Shipwreck at the Bottom of the World*, 10. A longer communication came later from Churchill encouraging them in their mission.

48. Ibid., 5, 7.

49. Quoted in Armstrong, *Shipwreck at the Bottom of the World*, 70.

50. Winston Churchill, "These Are Great Days: A Speech to the Boys of Harrow School, October 29, 1941," in his *The Unrelenting Struggle: War Speeches*, comp. Charles Eade (Boston: Little, Brown, 1942), 287.

51. See Shelby Foote, *The Civil War: A Narrative*, 3 vols. (New York: Alfred A. Knopf, 1986). Quoted by Joe Lieberman in Margaret Carlson, "Joe versus the Volcano," *Time* (18 December 2000), 49.

    See also http://academic.claremontmckenna.edu/jpitney/ice.htm and www.cnn.com/ALLPOLITICS/1996/conventions/san.diego/news/time.daily /0811.sh. . . . Accessed 25 February 2004.

Lend an Ear

Hear a Vision,
See the Sound

If you have ears to hear, then hear.

—Rabbi Jesus[1]

The story is told of a revered Chinese teacher known as "the Blind Master." On a beautiful spring day, the Blind Master was walking in the monastery garden with one of his students. As they passed near a large peach tree, the teacher moved his head to miss an overhanging limb. The pupil looked startled and asked, "Teacher, how is it that you saw that branch in front of you?" The Blind Master answered, "To see with the eye is only one sensation. I heard the wind sing softly in the tree's branches."

Naturalist John Muir could in the darkest nights pick out what type of conifer was in the canopy overhead by the singing of the wind in the reeds of the needles.

In 1999 Panasonic did a special three-page ad section called "Leonardo da Vinci: The Art of Seeing." It centered on da Vinci's philosophy, summed up in two words: *Saper vedere*, or "knowing how to see." What the advertising blitz failed to tell its readers was that da Vinci probably painted no more than 30 paintings in his entire lifetime, and fewer than half of those have come down to us. Da Vinci was able to impact the course of history with such a meager portfolio, not because of his powers of vision alone, but because his *saper vedere* philosophy presumed an ear to the ground, not a life at the grindstone.

Saper vedere presumed *Sapere aude:* "Dare to know" (Denis Diderot's badge). As art expert E. H. Gombrich (1909–2001) liked to point out, artists don't paint purely and simply what they see so much as they see what they paint.[2]

For "dreams" and "visions" to be prophecies, not memories, they need to be built from the sound up. A vision is something you *hear* on the horizon, not see. An odd expression in Exodus shows up in the Septuagint version: people "saw the voice of the Lord."[3] It appears again in Habakkuk 2:1: "Look to see what he will say." It is echoed in Revelation 1:12: "See the voice." In William Wharton's novel *Last Lovers*, there is a conclusion that "perhaps sometimes it is best to be blind, so one can see the way things really are, and not be blinded by the way they look."[4] Leadership is not first a "vision" thing. Leadership is first a "vibration" thing. The most important organ for a leader is the ears.

> What we see is dictated by what we hear.
> —The narrator in William Burroughs's novel *The Ticket That Exploded* [5]

Submarines have no windows. You can't "see" out. So how do you navigate a submarine? You "hear" your way forward. A submarine analyzes acoustic data from thousands of sensors and propels its way forward by sound guidance.

An old film about the laws of sound shows a handful of iron filings placed on a thin sheet of metal. A musical tone is played near the sheet. Suddenly the filings arrange themselves in the form of a snowflake. Sound becomes sight as vibrations take physical shape. Another tone is sounded, and the filings change their formation, this time into a star. Every note sounded creates its own physical form.

> Vision is the art of seeing things invisible.
> —Jonathan Swift (1667–1745)[6]

A HEARING HEART

The key to leadership is making the inaudible become audible and the invisible become visible. The initial mode of leadership is receptivity: hearing, not speaking. A hearing heart picks up signals rather in the way radio receivers pick up waves from the ether. In fact, sometimes you "hear" it from its absence as much as from its presence.

Note the choice of the word *hearing*, not *listening*. There is a difference. You can listen and not hear. Many people are "listened to"; few people are truly "heard." Hearing connects us to that which is unseen and unsaid.

Managers see into sound. Leaders hear into speech[7] and sight. When Saul of Tarsus was called from *managing* a problem to *leading* a people, he heard and heeded the voice that others could not interpret.

One of the greatest achievements of life is not a seeing mind but a hearing heart. The ears, not the eyes, are the gateway to leadership. Sight transforms the world into an object. Sound treats the world as a subject. Sight is distancing. Sound is enveloping. When visions are seen, paradoxically, reality is blinked. When visions are heard, leaders open themselves up to what the world needs and to new possibilities of truth. Jesus identified himself by what he heard: "what I have heard . . . I tell the world."[8]

Voice-activated leadership moves from vision to vibration, from eye to ear, from structure to rhythm. Instead of squinting at the future, perhaps we should keep our ears cocked and become "all ears." You are what you hear more than you are what you see.

We naturally prefer the eyes to the ears because when we look with our eyes we are in control of reality. In contrast to the millions of trademarked images, there is only a handful of trademarked sounds: for example, (1) the NBC Chimes, (2) the MGM lion, and (3) the Harley-Davidson "Hog" engine.[9] When we hear with our ears, we are vulnerable to reality.[10] Yet, as Katherine Hayles writes, "researchers in virtual

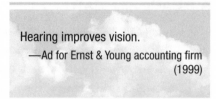

reality have found that sound is much more effective than sight in imparting emotional tonalities to their simulated words."[11]

What are the "soundmarks" of your church or business?

DISCERNING REALITY

With the eyes we can construct our own reality; with the ears we have to deal with situations as they really are. Of the five sense organs, only one is connected directly to the brain: the ear. We remember more musical melodies than we do prose passages because the brain is wired for sound more than sight.

A magician is nothing more than an illusionist who banks a professional reputation on the deceivability of the eyes. Eyes are easily fooled. That's why the "pinch test": Is it a real or artificial flower? To find out you pinch it. The eyes create "optical illusions" as quickly as you can drop a pencil into a glass of water or drive down a water-miraged highway.

You look different to everyone you meet. Every person who looks at you sees a different you. Why? Because "you" are data to the eyes, and each person's eyes organize data differently from others'. The constellation of stars North Americans call "the Big Dipper" the English call "the Plough." USAmerica sees "the man in the moon," but in China they see "the rabbit in the moon."

Forgetting for now Goethe's motto that "optical illusion is visual truth," we have eyelids for a reason—to block our eyes from tricking us. We don't have earlids for a reason: we can trust our ears (shaped like a question mark?) to test and discern reality.

Voice-activated leaders combine a designing eye with a discerning ear. In fact, *discern* comes from the Hebrew word that means "to hear." Hence the beginning of the capstone summation of Hebrew faith known as the *Schema*: "Hear, O Israel"—which is equally translated "Discern, O Israel"—"The LORD our God, the LORD is one. Love the LORD your God with all your heart and with all your soul and with all your strength."[12]

Peter Drucker once remarked that 60 percent of the problems in the workplace result from faulty communications. The percentages could only increase in regard to leadership, the very essence of which is communications. Why are communications sometimes so faulty? Too much designing eye; not enough discerning ear. The leader's lot is constant hearing, constant communication, and continuous feedback loops.

> If a sailor does not know to what port he is sailing, no wind is favorable.
>
> —Seneca

Ever wonder which is worse: To go blind like Milton (who wrote *Paradise Lost* when blind)? Or to go deaf like Beethoven (who wrote the *Ninth Symphony* when deaf)? Why not ask the expert? Blind/deaf/mute Helen Keller was convinced from a lifetime of experience that deafness is worse than blindness:

> I am just as deaf as I am blind. . . . Deafness is a much worse misfortune. For it means the loss of the most vital stimulus—the sound of the voice that brings language, sets thoughts astir and keeps us in . . . intellectual company. . . . I have found deafness to be a much greater handicap than blindness.[13]

We perceive more of the world with our ears than our eyes. Eyes grow a little from their size at birth, but not much. Our nose and ears never stop growing. Hearing is the first of the senses to greet us before we are born; hearing is the last of the senses to leave us at death. The ear is the only human sense organ that is able to perceive both numerical *quantity* and numerical *value*.[14] The "ear-gate"—so much more developed and sensitive than our "eye-gate"—has been created to act as the natural conduit of connection between creatures and creation.

HEARING A VISION

A leader's first task is hearing. Leaders don't "see" a vision. Leaders "hear" a vision. Sound becomes sight. Vibrations become visions. The voice arrests; the vision directs. In fact, some people who have perfect pitch actually hear in colors. That's why perfect pitch is also known as "color hearing."[16]

Sound travels in wave frequencies, and so does light. Speed up sound (i.e., the number of vibrations per second) or slow down light (i.e., the number of vibrations per second), and they become synonymous.

Leaders hear life. They hear other people. Yet so much of our time in the church context is spent talking, as if we can talk our way into leadership.

> A piece of music that I love expresses thoughts to me that are not too *imprecise* to be framed in words, but too *precise*. So I find that attempts to express such thoughts in words may have some point to them, but they are also unsatisfying.
>
> —Felix Mendelssohn[15]

When faced with a sanitation problem in their African village, the residents faced the issue first by drumming. Then they sang. Then they danced the chicken dance. After all that, they sat in silence and visualized the problem's "solution." As the Society of Friends have long taught, listening is not passive, but active. In the words of Quaker philosopher Scott Savage, "Friends use the 'technology' of *sitting*, the 'dialectic' of *waiting*, and the 'activist platform' of *listening*."[17]

How much time do you spend listening?

When asked how he came up with the design for his most famous residence, Fallingwater House in Bear Run, Pennsylvania, architect Frank Lloyd Wright replied,

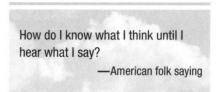

How do I know what I think until I hear what I say?

—American folk saying

"The visit to the waterfall in the woods stays with me and a domicile has taken vague shape in my mind to the music of the stream."[18] When asked to comment on a piece of music, tenor sax player Charles Lloyd once said, "Words don't go there."[19] According to Toni Morrison, black history was written above all in music.[20]

It is interesting how Hollywood storytellers Stephen Spielberg and George Lucas have captured the hearing essence of leadership. In *Jurassic Park*, when did the characters first know that T-Rex was about to appear? They felt and heard the vibrations. By the time they "saw" T-Rex, it was too late.

In the *Star Wars* trilogy, how did Luke Skywalker learn to lean into the power of the Force? Did he cultivate "the vision thing"? Hardly. He was tutored with blindfolding headgear to suppress his natural inclination to "look" and instead was trained to "hear" and "feel" the Force.

If you learned to drive a car with a clutch, you did so in the same way Luke Skywalker learned to pilot his save-the-world spacecraft. Amidst a lot of stalling out, grinding gears and rolling backwards, you were taught not to trust your eyes but to hear the hum of the engine, to sense the vibrations of the car, and to "feel" your way forward.

When hearing is good, speaking is good.

—Ancient Egyptian proverb

I am convinced we spend way too much time making noise rather than listening to the vibrations of the very people we are called to lead.

Cosmic vibrations are the surround sounds of the universe.[22] Sound is the energy formed by vibrations. Put sound and rhythm together and you get ...

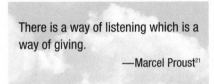

There is a way of listening which is a way of giving.

—Marcel Proust[21]

music. From our toes to our teeth, from hail to Hail Mary's, everything emits vibrations—sounds to feed or famish the soul. In Nadya Aisenberg's collection of poems there is a line about a land where

There are no words
but some notes Eve taught the birds.[23]

What language does nature speak? The language of sound. We live in an ocean of vibrations. Nothing is without music. If we don't know the meaning of the sounds, we can't interpret life. What to some is the voice of truth, to others is sheer racket. What to some is deafening thunder and lightning, to others is the voice of an angel. What to some is "bad luck" or "good fortune," to others is divine providence. When some hear "failure," others hear "success."

What do you hear when you listen? Your calling came from God, but now others are calling. How can you lead if you can't hear?

Poets used to talk about the "silence" of the deep oceans or the "stillness" of outer space. Now we know that all of creation hums the hymns of life. Everything that is has sound and rhythm—from oysters and ostriches to gallium arsenide and galaxies. Fin whales can easily hear the bleeps of other fin whales 4000 miles away; some scientists argue 13,000 miles away. Humpbacks often sing in rhyme, and the songs they sing are always changing while at the

A stone is frozen music.

—Pythagoras

---

same time they are passed from male to male "so that in any one season all the whales of a single ocean will be singing the same song."[24]

If it happens in the oceans, can it happen elsewhere? Is church too sterile for whale songs? What sounds like silence may be an ocean of sound brimming

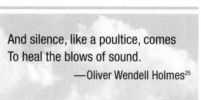

And silence, like a poultice, comes
To heal the blows of sound.
—Oliver Wendell Holmes[25]

to the surface in search of a leader who knows the difference.

CHANGING THE WAY YOU SEE

If you're without a vision, you're without a future. A vision *is* a future. Vision is not something you follow; it is the behest of hearing. Hearing is what gives vision. That's why one consultant, tired of visionaries acting like actuaries, has given up talking about "vision" and now uses the term "vow."

A vow is an intention to do something great that emerges from working out our purpose. It is not a specific goal or a targeted, idealized destination. It is a compulsion that suggests specific achievable things (objectives).[26]

When the National Museum of the American Indian component of the Smithsonian Institution opened, it announced its membership drive this way: "Any museum can invite you to look. A great one changes the way you see." To paraphrase French author Marcel Proust, "The real voyage of discovery consists not in seeking new lands, but in seeing with new eyes."[27]

Blessed is he who sees with his heart but whose heart is not in what he sees.
—Alleged Jesus saying[28]

Inventor Alan Kay's famous aphorism is that "a new point of view [or perspective] is worth 80 IQ points."[29] How do you "see"? What is your "orientation"? What direction do you

Lend an Ear

63

"face"? *Orient* means to face eastward, and that is the requirement today; the sun is rising in the East, both literally and figuratively.

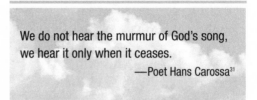

We do not hear the murmur of God's song, we hear it only when it ceases.
—Poet Hans Carossa[31]

As a wise man once said, it's more important to see what you see rather than know what you see. The best leaders, like the best poets, "impart the gift of seeing to the rest."[30]

SOUND LEADERSHIP

It's time church leaders developed a philosophy of soundness, even a sound spirituality.[32] The Greek word *cathecesis* is based on our word "echo." Could it be that our spirituality isn't as "sound" as it should be because we haven't understood sound as a way of experiencing the divine? Could it be that we do not "endure sound doctrine" because we do not "hold fast the pattern of sound words" from the divine soundscape?[33]

The beginning of the Bible is a hymn, a creation hymn. Some of Shackleton's favorite portions of Scripture were from the biblical hymnbook, the Psalms, many of which are musical love-poems to God. The Holy Book is one-third hymnbook. It could just as easily be called "the Holy Song." Genesis 1 *hymns* how God created the world:

All creation is a song of praise to God.
—Hildegard of Bingen

"Then God said, 'Let there be light'; and there was light."[34] Creation was a speech event. Creation was literally "sounded forth." Sound became sight. Cosmic vibrations became galactic visions. The cosmos began with a Sound.

Composer-conductor Leonard Bernstein came up with one of the best definitions of music ever uttered: "cosmos in the midst of chaos."[35] Bernstein was fond of pontificating from his conductor's perch that the best translation of the Hebrew in Genesis 1 was not "and God said" but "and God *sang.*" For this reason the original Hebrew text of the Pentateuch was read aloud—or more accurately, chanted. In fact, it is still often chanted in modern synagogues.

> Then God [sang], "Let there be light'; and there was light" (Genesis 1:3).
>
> Then God [sang] . . . and it was so (v. 9).
>
> Then God [sang] . . . and it was so (v. 11).
>
> Then God [sang] . . . and it was so (vv. 14–15 NASB).

Creation utters its own sounds, and scientists are still picking up those soundings. In fact, according to the most recent scientific findings, sound waves have shaped how the cosmos is structured. *Science News* offered this striking statement: "Sound waves generated in the early universe may have helped orchestrate the striking pattern of galaxy clusters and huge voids seen in the sky today."[36] Even a black hole sings . . . lower than the human ear can hear. The Perseus galaxy cluster sounds a strong bass note in the music of the spheres. The black hole's sounds waves create a long, constant B-flat, 57 octaves below middle C.

Once again, in other words—in *biblical* words: "Then God *sang,* 'Let there be light.' "

In deaf times the ear begins to hear. In the land of the deaf, it is necessary to shout. But not always. A leader's strength lies not just in his sounds but in his silences.

Sydney Smith said of the historian Thomas Babington Macaulay: "He has occasional flashes of silence which make his conversation delightful."[38]

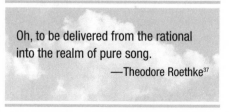

> Oh, to be delivered from the rational into the realm of pure song.
>
> —Theodore Roethke[37]

Perhaps one of the most "delightful" conversations in literature is the one three friends had with Job. They traveled from afar to sit with Job for three whole days . . . before speaking a word. Their simple adornment in sackcloth and ashes played a decibel level fit for their depressed and hurting friend.

In George Eliot's long novel *Middlemarch*, the narrator cautions that "if we had keen vision and feeling of all ordinary human life, it would be like hearing the grass grow and the squirrel's heart beat, and we should die of that roar which lies on the other side of silence. As it is, the quickest of us walk about well wadded with stupidity."[39]

David Anderson, rector of Trinity Church in Solebury, Pennsylvania, begins his book *Breakfast Epiphanies* with these words:

> Several years ago I ran into a friend at a dinner party. When I asked him how he was doing, he told me he'd had a tough day. "My car stalled on I–95 just out of town," he said, "and I had to wait an hour for a tow truck."
>
> Suddenly a scene flashed on my eye. "Oh," I said, "that was *you*—in the blue car? I was out there today and drove right past. I didn't really look—I just saw a car and someone standing there. If I'd known it was you, I would've stopped!"[40]

Anderson continues, "That pretty much sums up my search for God: If I'd known it was You, I would've stopped."

The faster everything moves—the greater the velocity of change—the more blurred our vision becomes. All the more reason to listen. A fast-changing culture demands the fine-tuned hearing of the blind. It is what enables a true leader to proceed even when he or she cannot see the whole picture.

We need both noise and silence in the soundscape of life. Without silence (read "peace and quiet"), we miss the subtleties of life that are drowned out by noise pollution, and the connections of mind, body, and spirit.

Leadership is sound management. Leaders create a sound environment.

SEEING THE MUSIC

Yousuf Karsh was a Canadian portrait photographer who spent 50 years taking pictures of some of the most famous people of the 20th century. The only picture he ever took of a person's back was of Pablo Casals in a small French abbey in 1954.

As Karsh was setting up his equipment, Casals began playing Bach on his cello. Karsh was so enthralled by the music that he almost forgot why he was there. In that moment of music, Karsh caught the picture of a tiny, bald-headed man bent over his cello, frozen in time against the aged stone of the chapel wall.

> You know something about the shape of the life you've chosen to live between the silence of almost infinite possibility and that explosion of things as they are.
>
> —Eamon Grennan[41]

When that portrait was on exhibition in the Museum of Fine Arts in Boston, the curator noticed another bald-headed, elderly man who came day after day and stood silently in front of it for long periods of time. Finally, the curator tapped the old man on the shoulder and asked him what he was doing. With obvious irritation, the old man turned to the curator and said, "Hush, young man! Can't you see I'm listening to the music?"[42]

Karsh heard Casals play Bach and caught the picture. The old man could hear the music by looking at the picture.

Can people hear the music by looking at you?

> Did you hear it?
>
> —Angel Nicholas Cage to human Dennis Franz as they "watch" a sunset in the movie *City of Angels* (1998)

SHACKLETON MODULATIONS:	In Tune • The Magic of Music

To "give ear" to anything—especially life—is to pay attention and learn. Shackleton experienced the world and learned as much with his ears as with his eyes. Attuned to the aural universe of the Antarctic, he listened to the soundscapes of nature, the vibrations in the air, the creaking of the ice, the voices of the animals. He could tell the world was different because it sounded different, and he studied the sounds to learn the difference.

> Hearing is the sense most favored by attention; it holds the frontier, so to speak, at the point where seeing fails.
>
> —Paul Valéry[43]

In Tune

The sounds of nature were the keys that unlocked Shackleton's navigation in the Antarctic. Just as a physician uses his stethoscope to hear inside the body, The Boss held a finger to his ear as an antenna to the changing soundscape. Or, as Shackleton put it: "We had seen God in his splendors and heard the text that Nature renders. We have reached the naked soul of man."[44]

His tuning in to the icy world about him was life-preserving. In the race to safety after the ice began breaking up, Shackleton and his men landed the three lifeboats on an ice floe for a night to avoid being crushed by ice in the dark.

Around 11 o'clock something "intangible" made The Boss get up and climb out of his tent. As he walked past another tent, the ice floe they were camped on split in two right beneath his feet—and under the open-bottomed tent. Peering into the darkness of the widening crack in the ice, Shackleton saw something. Plunging his hand into the icy water, he grabbed a sleeping bag still encasing a crewman and pulled him out.

Had Shackleton not sensed something amiss in the music of the ice, that crewman would likely have been lost.

The Magic of Music

If Shackleton was hard-edged, it was about only one thing: the importance of music to an expedition. He allowed on ship two gramophones and the meteorologist's banjo. He also allowed Thomas Crean to sing while steering at the tiller.

The Boss put together what were called "gramophone evenings." Only when the ship—locked in a death-grip of ice—seemed to creak and crack more when the records were playing did Shackleton ban these events. He paid homage to the power of music to alter reality, in this case by increasing the pressure of the ice on the ship.[45]

On October 25, 1915, The Boss ordered the lifeboats, equipment, and supplies off the disabled ship, which by now had listed 30 degrees to the side. Even though the ice pressure was mangling the hull, the crew still clung to a glimmer of hope for the craft. They knew they were in trouble, however, when they saw how Shackleton responded to the ominous drumbeat sounded by eight emperor penguins that appeared out of the fog and came waddling toward the ship. They stopped and just stood there, looking strangely at the disabled hull. Suddenly they tilted their heads to face upward and let out a forlorn howl. Similar penguins had been around regularly on the voyage, but they had been silent. It seemed to all who witnessed it that these penguins were sounding a dirge.

Two days later, Shackleton gave the order to abandon ship: "She's going, boys. I think it's time to get off." Raising the flag one last time on the battered mast, they began the evacuation.

Only the bare necessities were rescued from the crinkling vessel. "I brought your banjo ashore," Shackleton told Leonard Hussey, the ship's meteorologist, humorist, and musician. "It's vital mental medicine, and we shall need it."[46] Shackleton credited Hussey and his banjo as being a "vital factor in chasing away symptoms of depression."[47] To survive the impossible, his men would need two pills: story and song.

They would need the banjo for more reasons than a diversion to relieve tension. Music was the source of their salvation itself. With Hussey accompanying the crew's singing, even the initially skeptical photographer Frank Hurley would come to admit that music was "indispensable." And the resident pessimist, Thomas Ordes-Lee, added, "It really does, as Sir Ernest said, supply brain food."[48]

I have forgotten my guitar! I am losing my wits.

—Figaro

Shackleton encouraged his crew to sing together, and their ability to keep time with one another saved the day more than once. On board the three lifeboats, the men kept their rowing in rhythm by the foot-stomping drumbeat of those not rowing.

While waiting on Elephant Island for the rescue ship, dry-as-dust academician and physicist Reginald James composed a song for the occasion to honor his shipmate Frank Wild, who had been left in charge when Shackleton and five others sailed off to get help. Sung to the tune of "Solomon Levi," the chorus went:

My name is Frankie Wild-o, my hut's on Elephant Isle.

The wall's without a single brick, the roof's without a tile.

But nevertheless, you must confess, for many and many a mile,

It's the most palatial dwelling place you'll find on Elephant Isle.[49]

What beat are you drumming for others to follow?

NOTES

1. Mark 4:9 and 23 REB.
2. See, for example, E. H. Gombrich, *Art and Illusion: A Study in the Psychology of Pictorial Representation* (London: Phaidon Press, 1959), 258–59.

3. Exodus 20:18 Septuagint.
4. William Wharton, *Last Lovers* (New York: Farrar, Straus & Giroux, 1991), 36.
5. William Burroughs, *The Ticket That Exploded* (New York: Grove Press, 1967), 168.
6. Jonathan Swift, "Thoughts on Various Subjects" (1726) in his *A Proposal for Correcting the English Tongue, Polite Conversation, Etc.*, ed. Herbert Davis (Oxford: Basil Blackwell, 1964), 252.
7. The phrase "hear into speech" comes from former Drew University professor Nell Morton.
8. John 8:26 NIV.
9. To hear the NBC Chimes, check out www.kingoftheroad.net/KARD _html/bwchimes.html. For the MGM Roar, hear www.mgm.com/home.do and click on the small icon in the upper left corner of the window. For the Harley-Davidson Sound, hear www.bc.edu/bcorg/avp/law/st_org/iptf/articles/content/1998101101.html. For more "soundmarks" there is now a search engine to explore at www.findsounds.com.
10. Or as Lorenz Oken pointed out years ago, the eyes take us into the world whereas the ears take the world into us. Perhaps that is why Western religions have emphasized sacred time, sacred space, and sacred image over sacred sound. William F. Allman, in "The Dawn of Creativity" (*U.S. News & World Report* [20 May 1996], 56–57), reveals a unique feature to the cave art of Ice Age Europe: "Ice Age galleries may have been part of elaborate ceremonies that perhaps rivaled the best modern-day multimedia displays. Flutes made of bird bone that play notes in a scale similar to those of today suggest music may have accompanied viewing of the paintings. In one experiment, researchers walked through three ancient caves while whistling through several octaves and mapping where the sounds resonated off the walls best. They found that those places in the caves with the best acoustics nearly always had art nearby, whereas places where sound was dampened typically did not have art. In another experiment, researchers found that near the front of the famed Lascaux cave, where the cave art is dominated by horses, bison and other hoofed animals, a clapping noise gets echoed back and forth among the walls, producing a sound not unlike a stampede. Near the rear of the cave, however, where the images are dominated by panthers and other stealthy creatures, the walls reflect sound in such a way that it is muted."
11. N. Katherine Hayles, *How We Became Posthuman: Virtual Bodies in Cybernetics, Literature, and Informatics* (Chicago: University of Chicago Press, 1999), 219.
12. Deuteronomy 6:4–5 NIV.
13. Quoted in Jonathan Kramer and Diane Dunaway Kramer, *Losing the Weight of the World: A Spiritual Diet to Nourish the Soul* (New York: Doubleday, 1997), 119.
14. *Music and Aesthetics in the Eighteenth and Early Nineteenth Centuries*, ed. Peter le Huray and James Day (New York: Cambridge University Press, 1988), 135–36.
15. Quoted in *Music and Aesthetics*, ed. Le Huray and Day, 311.
16. David L. Burge begins his book *Perfect Pitch: Color Hearing for Expanded Musical Awareness* (Presque Isle, MI: Innersphere Music Studio, 1983) with the

chapter "There's Color in Your Ear!" (9). He writes, "To the *color ear*, the entire pitch spectrum is a dazzling display of distinct sound colors which dance within their musical framework and blend in various ways to form the different chords and tonalities" (12).

17. Scott Savage, *The Plain Reader: Essays on Making a Simple Life* (New York: Ballantine, 1998).

18. As quoted in Neil Levine, *The Architecture of Frank Lloyd Wright* (Princeton, NJ: Princeton University Press, 1996), 227.

19. As quoted by Bart Schneider, "Crossing the Alley," *Hungry Mind Review* (Fall 1993), 42.

20. Toni Morrison, *The Bluest Eye* (New York: Washington Square Press, 1984), 125.

21. As quoted in Ralph Harper, *On Presence* (Philadelphia: Trinity Press International, 1991), 43.

22. Harper, *On Presence,* 59. See also Chet Raymo, *The Virgin and the Mousetrap: Essays in Search of the Soul of Science* (New York: Viking, 1991), 156.

23. Nadya Aisenberg, "The Body against the Body," in *Before We Were Strangers: Poems* (Boston: Forest Books, 1989), 62.

24. Stephen Mills, "The Rhyming Whale," review of Roger Payne, *Among Whales* (1996), *TLS: Times Literary Supplement* (6 September 1996), 36.

25. Oliver Wendell Holmes, "The Music Grinders," in *The Poetical Works of Oliver Wendell Holmes* (Boston: Houghton, Mifflin, 1895), 10.

26. Kirk Hadaway, *Behold I Do a New Thing: Transforming Communities of Faith* (Cleveland: Pilgrim Press, 2001), 20.

27. The way Proust said it is, "The real voyage of discovery consists not in seeking new landscapes but in having new eyes."

28. A quote from Jesus according to *The Muslim Jesus: Sayings and Stories in Islamic Literature,* ed. Tarif Khalidi (Cambridge, MA: Harvard University Press, 2001), 106.

29. For more quotes from Kay, who invented the computer graphical user interface (GUI), see http://c2.com/cgi/wiki?AlanKayQuotes. Accessed 27 November 2002.

30. Robert Browning, "Sordello," in *The Complete Works of Robert Browning,* ed. Roma A. King (Athens, OH: Ohio University Press, 1970), 2:223.

31. As quoted in Hans-Georg Gadamer, *The Enigma of Health: The Art of Healing in a Scientific Age* (Stanford, CA: Stanford University Press, 1996), 3.

32. The concept of "sonic theology" in Guy L. Beck, *Sonic Theology: Hinduism and Sacred Sound* (Columbia: University of South Carolina Press, 1993), is based on the premise that knowledge is founded on more than visual "observation"; it is also based on oral and sonic sources. Beck laments the "growing impasse in the current study of human culture, a deadlock brought on by an overdependence on visual sources leading to a virtual neglect of what may be 'undescribed' or 'unseen.' Grappling with the seemingly Western obsession with the notion of empirical evidence, concerned writers have indicated that the emphasis on 'visualism' in Western thought reflects a deeper 'ideological bias toward vision as the "noblest sense" and toward geometry *qua* graphic-spatial conceptualization as the most exact way of communicating

knowledge . . . inherited . . . from rationalist thought [Descartes] and from the empiricists [Hobbes and Locke]'" (1).

For intellectuals' difficulty in taking music on its own terms, see Marshall Brown's failed attempt at a nonmusical definition of music: "Music is, undeniably, relationships and not sounds, the perfection of utterance and not visceral feeling, not the channeling or taming of noise but the intellectual word that manifests the silent pulse of being" (Marshall Brown, "Unheard Melodies: The Force of Form," in *Turning Points: Essays in the History of Cultural Expressions* [Stanford, CA: Stanford University Press, 1997], 264). With that last "silent pulse of being" he gave it all away.

33. 2 Timothy 4:3; 1:13 NKJV.
34. Genesis 1:3 NASB.
35. As quoted by Madeleine L'Engle, "Cosmos from Chaos," in her *Walking on Water: Reflections on Faith and Art* (New York: North Point Press, 1995), 17.
36. Ron Cowen, "Sound Waves May Drive Cosmic Structure," *Science News* (11 January 1997), 21.
37. Theodore Roethke, "What Can I Tell My Bones," in his *Words for the Wind: The Collected Verse of Theodore Roethke* (Garden City, NY: Doubleday, 1958), 211.
38. Sydney Smith, *A Memoir of the Reverend Sydney Smith by His Daughter Lady Holland and with a Selection from His Letters*, ed. Mrs. Austin (New York: Harper, 1855), 1:320.
39. George Eliot, *Middlemarch* (Boston: Dana Estes, n.d.), 1:203.
40. David Anderson, *Breakfast Epiphanies* (Boston: Beacon Press, 2002), ix.
41. Eamon Grennan, *Selected and New Poems* (New York: Gallery Books, 2001), as quoted in John Greening's "In Brief" review of Eamon Grennan, *Selected and New Poems*, *TLS: Times Literary Supplement* (20 April 2001), 37.
42. With thanks to James A. Harnish for this story: "Journey into Joy: Elizabeth and Zechariah–The Song of Hope," Hyde Park United Methodist Church in Tampa, Florida, 3 December 2000. See also Amanda Hopkinson, "Yousuf Karsh," *Guardian Unlimited* (15 July 2002). www.guardian.co.uk/obituaries/story/0,3604,755227,00.html.
43. Paul Valéry, *Analecta*, in his *Analects*, trans. Stuart Gilbert (Princeton, NJ: Princeton University Press, 1970), 270.
44. Ernest Shackleton, *South: The Endurance Expedition* (reprint, New York: Signet, 1999), 226.
45. Jennifer Armstrong, *Shipwreck at the Bottom of the World: The Extraordinary True Story of Shackleton and the Endurance* (New York: Crown, 1998), 42.
46. Roland Huntford, *Shackleton* (New York: Atheneum, 1985), 472.
47. As quoted in ibid., 538.
48. Ernest Shackleton, *South: The Story of Shackleton's 1914–1917 Expedition* (London: Heinemann, 1970), 144.
49. Armstrong, *Shipwreck at the Bottom of the World*, 121.

chapter 3

I Hear You

*Hire Good Vibrations
and Tune Your Team*

> If you want to build a ship, don't drum up the men to
> gather wood, divide the work, and give orders. Instead,
> teach them to yearn for the vast and endless sea.
>
> —Antoine de Saint Exupéry, "Make Me a Boat"[1]

One of the great challenges facing church leaders is finding the right people to join you in mission. Whether hiring paid staff or recruiting the right volunteers, your leadership is never more important than in building the right team for ministry.

In the first chapter we looked at the incredible Power of One, the biblical truth—often ignored—that one person can indeed change the world.

The key to the Power of One, however, is two. When the number one is multiplied to the nth power, it is still one. One to the 100th power is still one.

But two to the 100th power is astronomical. The Power of One is nothing without another.[2] The Power of One is powerless without a team.

The current view of team leadership is that the team listens to the leader and follows. The soundful leader, however, turns that upside down:

"I hear you."

These are the three greatest words a team can hear from an acoustic leader.

In this chapter I hope to challenge your view of team building. So much of what passes for "ministry teams" is based on faulty principles. We look for the best and brightest instead of listening to the spirit.

HIRING GOOD VIBRATIONS

A new mantra is making the rounds of corporate life today: "Hire attitude and aptitude. Train for skill."

More important than finding someone to fill a "job description" is hiring an employee with the right "spirit description." In the past, leaders "placed" people in positions the way Ford production workers "placed" parts in cars on assembly lines. People who "knew their place" and would "stay in place" were promoted up the factory floor and pushed up the corporate ladder.

The awareness is dawning, however, that great leadership is less trying to find people to "fit in" than finding people who can "fit together."[3] In others words, better to start with a spirit description than a job description. Better to conduct job inner-views before job inter-views. In a world that works in circles— "what goes around, comes around"—inner circles are less to be squared than squired. When it comes to teams, circles are virtuous, not vicious.

Jack Kobuskie, my high school basketball coach in Gloversville, New York, used to tell us that he wanted to play his best five, not his five best.

Choose to play your best team.

A Right Spirit

The ultimate in matters of right and wrong are right spirits and wrong spirits. Matters of good and bad employees come down to those with good attitudes and those with kinks of spirit. One employee with a "toxic" attitude[4] can slow down if not bring down an entire corporation. Bad vibrations can demolish an organization as fast as bad vibrations toppled the Tacoma Narrows Bridge on November 7, 1940.[5]

Then there's the prop-jet Electra, which had one unfortunate design flaw: the rhythms of its rotating propellers matched the natural frequency of the wings. In other words, the airplane would resonate with itself and self-destruct. Talk about bad vibrations!

To build any endeavor on "principles" or "policy" is shaky ground and sinking sand. Set up all the principles you want, and one leader with a corrupt spirit or bad attitude can destroy all those "principles" in three months.[6]

The growing recognition of the dangers of a "bad spirit" can be seen in the way more and more companies are firing clients and contractors. Some companies have made it "company policy" to sign contracts and keep contractual relationships going only with pleasant people. Clients with bad attitudes and demanding, disrespectful dispositions are being told, "We don't want your money," and are fired.[7]

Nothing sinks a ship faster than negativity. Nothing kills faster than the poison brew of pessimism. Some people go through spring and see azaleas and peonies; others see "nature's bad mood" when "buds burst like infected wounds."[8] Which would you rather be around? For some people, the sounds of romance are roses opening and violins playing. For others, romance means "I will find that special person who is wrong for me in just the right way."[9] Which one would you rather spend an evening with?

Negativity can be both structural and personal. We tend to focus on negative people, but some organizational climates create negativity through back-biting, backstabbing, scape-goating, and sabotage.

You can trust the spirit more than you can trust the process or the policy

> If I had my life to live over, I would start barefoot earlier in the spring and stay that way later in the fall.
>
> —Octogenarian poet Nadine Stair[10]

or the resumé. Values, mission statements, rules of efficiency—none of these make or break successfulness. A person's—or an organization's—spirit does.

After the Great Corporate Meltdown of 2002, does anyone think that lofty "core principles" lift up a company to either integrity or profitability? Enron was lauded as a model corporate citizen. Enron's CEO Kenneth Lay gave speeches on ethics at corporate conferences, where his potboiler quote was "The responsibility of our board—a responsibility which I expect them to fulfill—is to ensure legal and ethical conduct by the company and by everyone in the company. . . . It is the most important thing we expect from board members."[11] Enron plastered its ethics program on T-shirts, coffee mugs, banners, everything: RICE (Respect, Integrity, Community, Excellence).

Or take Arthur Andersen. It hired an ethics expert in 1995 to create a corporate-ethics consulting practice for the firm. There was only one problem: the ethics programs she developed for clients were never implemented by Arthur Andersen itself. All her attempts to get the accounting firm to do so were rejected.[12]

What was missing in Enron and Arthur Andersen? Not "core principles," but core relationships. Did any of the corporate scoundrels need more rules? They had rules in place; they knew the rules; they professed to live by the rules. But their relationships flouted the rules.

Higher principles don't guarantee higher behavior. Only the right spirit does.

The fundamental ingredient voice-activated leaders look for in building a team is spirit. Spirit comes first. Spirit is the one nonnegotiable. Who would you be better off hiring? Someone who has all the job skills anyone could ask but gives off bad vibrations? Or someone who has minimal expertise and little or no experience but whose heart gives off such good vibrations that everyone likes to be around them and draws strength from their heartbeat?

Every soul sounds forth vibrations. The soul is music, and the body is the pipe organ of the soul. Everyone is musical. We don't make music so much as music makes us. Bad vibrations create health and social problems, low morale, and a host of other human resource nightmares. Good vibrations promote harmony, high energy, and a low turnover rate. A person's vibrations affect everything.

The hospitality industry is already in the throes of transitioning from an ideal of perfect execution to one of perfect attitude. Where would you rather stay? At a hotel whose operations run with clocklike efficiency, or one with a little less mechanical efficiency but whose staff is caring, anxious to please ("my pleasure"), and always trying to do the right thing for the guests?

> I believe that the invisible and the sword of the spirit could and *shall* make the bayonet and the machinegun impossible.
>
> —Novelist Marianne Moore[13]

In one year Four Seasons Hotels and Resorts saved $35,000 in each of its 37 hotels by not putting out chocolate each evening. They found that it wasn't all that big a deal to its guests. What was a big deal was the hiring of an extra person to give guests more customized, personalized attention.

We used to think greatness came from outside—power, position, prestige, wealth. We now know greatness comes from within—spirit, character, loyalty, honesty, soul. To paraphrase a Greek philosopher from the third century BC, "Money opens all gates, including the gates of hell."[14]

The most influential business newsletter in the world, *Trend Letter*, did a special feature on "Into the Spirit World" because of the "growing number of companies and individuals [who] are melding spirituality and religion into their business and professional undertakings."[15] Whether this represents "a sweeping trend from materialism to spirituality" remains to be seen. What it does signify is a growing sensitivity to the spirit realm as a foundation and not a scaffold. *Trend Letter* highlighted a couple of places for businesses to offer new products and services, and encouraged "advertising campaigns with spiritual themes," "educational programs with spiritual topics," and even "training for individuals pursuing spiritually related careers."

Four careers were specifically mentioned:

1. "Spiritual healers," which *Trend Letter* called "a major health care trend for the 21st century"
2. "Spiritual counselors," people who function outside religious institutions. (By 1998 there were 4000 "corporate chaplains," according to the National Institute of Business and Industrial Chaplains.)
3. "Spiritual business consultants," who help companies realize that "religious values can be good for the bottom line"
4. "Spiritual advisers" (already used by Lucent Technologies and the World Bank), who help employees deal with morale, personal problems, and spirituality[16]

What is the ultimate in a "right spirit"? Two components: confidence and humility. Or in their cognate forms, absolute concentration and total relaxation, gravity of purpose and levity of tone.

In Jim Collins's 1996 study of 1,435 companies that appeared on the Fortune 500 list from 1965 to 1995, only 11 made the truly "great" category. What "great companies" had in common was leaders who keep distinct, even opposing views and virtues without collapsing them into one another. Collins describes such leaders as "modest and willful, shy and fearless."[17] These people "look in the mirror" to apportion blame for poor performances and "look out the window" to credit success.

These leaders have ambition, "first and foremost for the company and concern for *its* success rather than for [their] own riches and personal renown."[18] Right-spirited leaders aren't afraid either to cut their hero cake or to eat their humble pie.

If this is a trend in the corporate world, what does it say to the church? Shouldn't *we* be the experts at placing ultimate value on the spiritual dimension? Yet so much of what I see in church leadership still appears to be rearranging the chairs.

Confidence

The confident leader embodies good energy, a sense of destiny, and a restless independence of mind. Arrogance is not confidence; confidence is not arrogance.

Alexander Hamilton introduced the concept of "energy" in *The Federalist* papers (1788). He connected energy with responsibility and republican safety: The responsible person is energetic, restless, not averse to risk, but with movements well-controlled. In other words, confident.

Hamilton called "energy" the leading characteristic of good government, especially in the executive branch. Replace the word *energy* with *confidence* and you have a fairly good understanding of the right-spiritedness of a confident leadership. A leadership crisis is another name for an energy crisis.

Is your leadership crisis really a lack of energy?

The first ingredient in energy is unity. A one-person executive allows for "decision, activity, secrecy, and dispatch"; unity in the executive is better than dispersed, disordered plurality.[19] In addition, you can hold one person accountable, but not a committee; you can watch one person carefully, but one can hide in a committee. As comedian Groucho Marx once said of his brother Harpo, "He's honest, but you've got to watch him."

The second ingredient in energy, according to Hamilton, is duration. Duration consists of steadfastness of focus and endurance of direction. Having the ability to make decisions, keeping the wants of the people in mind but not giving public opinion an infallible status, and limiting duration to four years—all these focusing energies, Hamilton said, give a sense of urgency and firmness.[20]

The third ingredient of energy is adequate provision for its support. The executive must be paid well enough, but not too well. He must be free from temptations to be persuaded toward something simply for the sake of increasing his salary.[21] An executive must be taken care of if she is to care for her charge.

The fourth requisite of energy is competent powers. A leader needs to be granted the authority and power needed to accomplish any task. He dare not have absolute power, but without the appropriate power, there will be no energy in the leader.[22]

Humility

When leaders are called forth, they don't so much "rise" to the occasion as "bow" to the invitation. Voice-activated leaders undergo periodic ego audits.

Pro basketball star Joe Dumars jokes, "I've gotten so much attention for being underrated, I've become overrated."

Jim Collins argues that successful companies espouse grace, humility, gratitude, and honesty.

"Humility is not another word for hypocrisy; it is another word for honesty," says English pastor John R. W. Stott. "It is not pretending to be other than we are, but acknowledging the truth about what we are."[23]

Leaders in the corporate world are looking for cheerfulness and natural modesty, things that promote team spirit. Yet we in the church seem more fascinated with issues of competence, skill sets, and training.

Today we are moving from mechanistic organizations to organic organisms. Companies no longer thrive on the mechanistic principles of chain of command, job descriptions, and hierarchical structure. Instead, what works is a more organic system of musicking performances that sound the keynotes of self-control, networks, speed, and relationship.

Taking Risks

Risk awareness first emerged in the Renaissance mercantile world, when the hazards of sailing were discussed among tradesmen in Italy and Spain in the 15th century. Sailors had to take risks, and owners insured the lives of sailors and the value of their goods.[24]

It used to be the contrasts were between risk and refuge. Today the contrast is between risk and danger. "Risk management" is an oxymoron. Risk is a short name for movement. The road to wisdom and mission is not straight. It is a hazardous, haphazard road.

When ornithologist Amotz Zahavi proposed his "handicap principle" in the 1970s—"something can be good because it's bad"—it became almost a laughingstock in many circles. But the handicap principle that states that birds (and humans) survive not in spite of risk but because of it is an essential element of leadership. Leaders have to pay a significant cost, or handicap, to ensure the survival of the team.[25]

Jungian "soul-making" psychoanalyst James Hillman distinguishes between the soul and the spirit. The soul is that dimension of our being that revolves around depth and deals with depth issues. By contrast, spirit has more to do with height.[26] Spirit is about the Phoenix rising up from the ashes; soul is about honoring the ashes. Spirit wants to climb the mountain. Soul wants to enter the depths of the earth and plumb and plummet the meaning of relationships.

For the development of a team, spirit is more important than compatibility of vision and conformity of thought. It is a spirit that can share risks and endure them together.

I admire people whose papers are all "in order." But most of us have papers that aren't; they're still being assembled and assorted. In that setting up and sorting, people must be allowed to take risks. Success will not come without failures. When you have people with the right spirit, support them even when they make mistakes. People have a failure of nerve because they don't have the nerve of failure.[27]

In the Jewish Talmud's reflections on the Genesis account of creation, the rabbis deduced that God the Creator practiced on twenty-six unsuccessful universes before finding exactly the right combination. "On the 27th try, God supposedly said, 'Let's hope it works!'"[28]

Too often we build our teams with the wrong people and then release them for the wrong reasons. There are only three reasons for firing anyone. First, for not being fired up. Second, for not having a right spirit (which always backdrops subversive actions). Third, not for making mistakes, but for either making no mistakes or not learning from them.[29] Like a tree that nourishes itself on its own death, leaders find strength from their mistakes and failures.

> In times of rapid change, experience is our worst enemy.
> —Attributed to business tycoon J. Paul Getty

Too many people, as a wag once put it, do not have thirty years' experience, but rather one year's experience thirty times. Our experience can also become an albatross hanging from our necks. We even need to be humble about the value of our experience. All our experience deals with the past, yet all our problems and challenges are of the future. In the words of Michael Marquardt, "Existing knowledge tends to misdirect rather than facilitate problem resolution."[30]

TUNE YOUR TEAM

Jennifer Rubell, co-owner of Rubell Hotels, has the job title of "Director of Vibe." Her job is to "intensify the vibe." When asked what a good vibe feels like, she responds, "It's a feeling of warmth, playfulness."[31] Coordinated rhythmical activity is fundamental to team life and health.[32]

Wouldn't it be great if the senior pastor became the "director of vibe"?

A leader forms a team based on spirit, but then the task becomes a constant fine-tuning to keep everyone on the same wavelength. Musicking is a group experience. Rituals offer space in which people can mold and morph themselves into each other and thereby reset their relationships and more harmonious interactions within the group. Leadership can almost be defined as the never-ending quest for the Lost Chord.

Recent research has reinforced Richard Condon's hypothesis that behavior is a wave phenomenon reflecting the deep human desire for harmony. As social creatures we pick up signals from each other and mutually regulate our body states. Such group-synchronized neurodynamics were demonstrated by slaves singing in the fields, their minds synchronized into a single dynamic system of interacting brains and bodies.

Studies by Kent State University sociologists Stanford Gregory and Stephen Webster reveal that productive conversations require that speakers be literally "on the same wavelength." After studying 25 interviewees from the *Larry King Live* talk show, paying particular attention to the low-frequency tones below 500 herz, Gregory and Webster discovered that one person would set the tone and the other would modulate frequencies to match. With high-status guests, King would shift levels. Low-status guests would defer to King's wavelength. In duplicating these results elsewhere, Gregory and Webster theorize that these matching "undertones" constitute a nonverbal form of communication by which we unconsciously manage "dominance-deference relations."[33] The low humming beneath our words seems to be, as one anthropologist put it, "an elaborate code that is written nowhere, known by none, and understood by all."[34]

In scientific laboratories we are finding that sound, harmony, rhythm, light, color, form, dance, and images all have an impact on human physiology and longevity. Music's capacity to reduce anxiety and pain is no longer debated.

Could it be that musicking is a *sound* thing to do? Literally? Physically and spiritually?

> Listen, for the life of your soul is at stake.
>
> —Isaiah 55:3 NLT

We make music for two reasons: to create pleasure and to alleviate anxiety.[35] Studies have shown that music lessens the trauma of separation anxiety in baby chicks; they cry less when they hear music.[36] Music can also, according to the American Music Therapy Association,

1. Reduce stress
2. Support physical exercise
3. Assist with child labor in delivery
4. Alleviate pain in conjunction with anesthesia or pain medication
5. Elevate mood and counteract depression
6. Promote movement for physical rehabilitation
7. Calm, sedate, or induce sleep
8. Counteract apprehension and fear
9. Lessen muscle tension
10. Increase physical, mental, social, and emotional functioning
11. Improve communication skills and physical coordination skills[37]

The story is told of the ancient Greek scientist Pythagoras of Samos (560–480 BC). As the shadows lengthened, he made his way down some narrow, cobblestone streets cradling his lyre and strumming on its string the music of the spheres. Suddenly the light of a rising moon reflected a steely glint off the blade of a dagger wielded by an assassin hiding in a darkened doorway. With a bloodcurdling scream, the man leaped from the darkness.

Pythagoras whirled to face his assailant. Instead of meeting him in mortal combat, Pythagoras began to play a piece of music on the lyre. The haunting strains cut deep into the soul of the would-be assassin. He dropped the knife and fell sobbing to his knees, overcome in a torrent of emotion.

When was the last time you asked your staff to sing at a staff meeting? To listen to your church's rhythms rather than trying to set the rhythm with yet another scheduled activity? Your team looks to you not so much for guidance but for inspiration. For spirit. For life.

Harmonious Difference

We all know we need team members who are different from us. Many today tend to talk in terms of diversity. I prefer to use the language of "difference" rather than "diversity": diversity has become an ideology, while difference is an ideal.

To allow difference is to smash conformity and allow the dignity of variety.

Difference is not just about race or gender or culture—that's diversity. It's also about multiplicities within yourself, throughout your life journey, around yourself.

A counterpoint rhythm can be beautiful when independent voices remain in harmony with one another.

It's been found that creative people tend to take varied routes to and from places they go regularly. Why? Difference is a chief preserver of creative vitality. Liberate your team's store of creativity and wisdom. When everyone and everything are the same all the time, creative people begin dying inside. Poet Les Murray calls creativity "the wound you receive in childhood that never heals"[38] and makes you different.

Difference means having a heart big enough to find room for rich and poor, conservative and liberal. Harmonious difference is what leaders everywhere need to seek more of today. There is an old monastic saying that argues for compassion and understanding in the following way: "Even the just man falls seven times a day." If that's the best that the best of us can do, we ought to be patient with one another.

We need each other: not just this other and that other, but *each* other. *Every* other.

The key question of church leadership in putting together a team of harmonious difference is this: "When they look at us, can they find themselves?"

In the 17th century an edict was passed by the Lord Protector of England, Oliver Cromwell, initiating a procedure to curtail the savage practices of some of his troops (ranging from rape to pillage and murder). The offending soldier and his entire company would assemble underneath the local gallows and hold a meeting. This meeting would consist of the rolling of dice. Everyone would participate. The man who lost would be hanged—not necessarily the instigator of the crime, but simply the man who lost. The result of this edict was fewer crimes and fewer meetings.

Even though we didn't all come over in the same ship, as the saying goes, we are all in the same boat—"poor, benighted members of the same ship's company," as Adlai Stevenson put it.

Management consultant Mark Sanborn says that "holographic teamwork" is where "the code of the entire team must reside within each member." This means a "shared understanding."[39] Different but harmonious.

Unfortunately, most church leaders waste opportunity by building teams that look like themselves. The next time you have an opening on your staff, make a list of all the places you would normally look to fill that slot. Then look everywhere else but there.

The Primacy of Relationship

The essence of leadership is relationship: influencing people to achieve things together that can't be achieved alone.

"Sonic leadership" is the rhythmic sounding of difference into organic wholeness—the musicking of polyvocal groups and the finding of keynotes that enables them to sound forth together in a common score. Such musicking performances are required whether you are trying to figure out where the office is going to order lunch or working with a divided board on whether to purchase a rival company ... at three times your

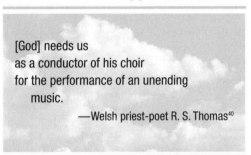

[God] needs us
as a conductor of his choir
for the performance of an unending
music.
　　　—Welsh priest-poet R. S. Thomas[40]

earnings.[41] The whole of this rhythmic sounding is greater than the simple sum of its individual processes and parts.

What happens in a work team? Think about this description of a "self-organizing system":

> A collection of random material entities that come together suddenly and begin to act as a single organism. These "complex systems" develop a remarkable adaptive capacity that allows them to shift on a dime in response to critical changes in their immediate environment. They also exhibit a paradoxical combination of order and freedom. Often there is a recognizable pattern to their behavior, but they are also capable of totally unpredictable conduct. So these systems thrive at "the edge of chaos," that fine line between their collective order and the freedom of their individual parts. If there is too much order in the system, then routinization, stagnation, and death will follow. If there is too much freedom, then anarchy, discord, and chaos result. Therefore, the critical life force within every complex natural system is this dynamic *balance between order and freedom*.[42]

The word *canon* sounds very academic. However, it actually comes from the same word as *cane*, as in the "caning" of chairs. Cane was a reed on the banks of the Nile and was used as a measuring rod, a way of establishing standards. Hence *canon* became synonymous with sound judgment. That is what is needed to keep the delicate balance between order and freedom.

Sir Ernest Shackleton demonstrated a set canon. He didn't impose a lot of rules; more important in the balance he kept were his sound judgments and rhythmic regimes.

In the words of Peter Keostenbaum, who has created a philosophy of leadership,

> Taking personal responsibility for getting others to implement strategy is the leader's key polarity. It's the existential paradox of holding yourself 100 percent responsible for the fate of your organization, on the one hand, and assuming absolutely no responsibility for the choices made by other people, on the other hand. That applies to your children too. You are 100 percent responsible for how your children turn out. And you accomplish that by teaching them that *they* are 100 percent responsible for how they turn out. So how do you motivate people? Not with techniques, but by risking yourself with a personal, lifelong commitment to greatness— by demonstrating courage.[43]

K. C. Jones was a pro basketball coach notorious for encouraging his players. But according to Boston Celtics forward Kevin McHale, Jones wouldn't slap a player on the back after he had made a great play. McHale once asked Coach Jones why he never congratulated his players after an outstanding performance. "Kevin," he said, "after you've made the winning basket, you've got 15,000 people cheering for you. TV commentators come rushing toward you. Everybody is giving you 'high fives.' You don't need *me* then. When you need a friend most is when nobody is cheering."

The true leader makes each team member twice the person they were before.

Trust is an essential element of relationship. Trust your team; believe in your players. In the words of writer/poet Robert Musil, "Man is a being that can no more stand up to suspicion than tissue-paper can stand up to rain."[44]

A leader faces fears in an attitude of faith. When Shackleton's ship was caught in the grip of ice, he knew that even more dangerous was being caught in the grip of fear.

Within that relationship of trust, a leader gives leadership away. The secret is to lift up others, not yourself. Empower people to learn, grow, think for themselves, and discover their own solutions. Mentor them. All of us have had mentors. All of us need them.

Give up asking, "Who's your boss?" Instead, start asking, "What's your team?"

Collaboration

A complaint I hear of church leaders is that they too often go it alone, getting way ahead (or remaining far behind) those they are trying to lead. What followers want—and what helps make a leader great—is collaboration.

The key to collaboration is simultaneity. In a leadership context, "simultaneity" means bringing people to the table who see things from a variety of perspectives: as women, as ethnic minorities, as the poor, even as the white males from whom we so often hear. The goal is not to duke it out until one perspective "wins" over the others; neither is the goal to meld all the perspectives into a blended, mushy soup. Rather, the goal is to learn to see things from many perspectives simultaneously by listening to one another. This kind of collaboration is sorely lacking in the church.

We need transparent leaders. Leaders who don't pretend to be who they aren't. Leaders who show compassion and respect for others. Leaders who act out of transparent goals. Leaders whom people trust and who trust people. Leaders who make everyone feel important.

"Leadership is a dance," according to Thomas Hawkins. "The partners in this dance are not rigidly divided into those who lead and those who follow. These dance partners do not need to hold onto one another. . . . dance partners can also change roles quickly and effortlessly. Now arm in arm; now face to face. Sometimes leading; sometimes following."[45]

A team is a complex tangle of relationships, sentiments, traditions, and roles. We collaborate in circles, not just between singular individuals. Finding the right "fit" no longer means finding someone who will "fit in" but people who will "fit together." Alliances and collaborative efforts are often for a brief period of time, for the accomplishment of a single task. Because of that, the "diplomatic art of managing ad hoc partnerships and alliances will become a key executive skill."[46]

Shackleton didn't save for himself the spacious corner office or other perks of power. He saved for himself the worst coat, or took the same as everyone else; he didn't wear warmer clothes than anyone else. He saw what things looked like from the crew's perspectives. His crew knew he cared about them.

Collaboration goes beyond tribe or nation and extends to the globe. Every serious investor today needs three brokers: one each in North America, a European financial center (London, Zurich, Luxemburg), and an Asian center (Hong Kong, Singapore, Tokyo).

Collaboration isn't only with other humans, but also with animals and machines: "The only items that account for a greater share of the household operations budget [than computers] are telephone equipment and services (average $909); furniture ($387); and day care ($232). The average household spends more on computer technology than on major appliances, lawn and gardening, or housewares."[47]

"We are moving rapidly towards one billion connected computers," Craig Barrett, Intel's chief executive, said in 1999. "This does not just represent an online community: it represents the formation of a 'virtual' continent."[48]

A networked world changes how people interact with each other. With a web connection, you can go from here to everywhere. You can collaborate across oceans with people you've never met, through machines you don't understand, to do business that's never been done before. Genuinely new forms of human relationships are being formed in cyberspace. These new forms are not computer-based, but are interactive, cyberspatial, dynamic, collaborative.

Nordstrom's is one of the more successful retail chains in the country. Why? John Nordstrom has no desk. The whole store is his desk. And he has a personal rule. The rule can be seen every time he walks up to an employee. No one shrinks back from him; instead, they are glad to see him. Why? Because he tries to find a reason to compliment an employee every day. And if he can't find a reason, he doesn't say anything negative. If he really can't find a reason, he gets rid of the employee.

Why ask people to join your team if you can't celebrate their work?

SHACKLETON MODULATIONS:	Reading Souls • Taking Risks • Blessings • Building a Team

The *Endurance* expedition took four years of planning, yet Shackleton chose the team members in lightning-quick speed.

Reading Souls

One of the questions the Boss asked a candidate had nothing to do with polar skills: Can you sing? "Oh, I don't mean any Caruso stuff, but at supper can you stat a bit with the boys?"[49] Shackleton picked his crew from over 5000 applicants—

including three young women.[50] Some thought Shackleton was too capricious and whimsical in his interviews. He sized up someone intuitively and very quickly, asked a few leading questions to tease out something about their mettle, and then made an immediate decision. Shackelton had confidence in himself. He had a sense that he wasn't the only stick in God's matchbox, but it was his stick God had chosen to light the fire.

> Men Wanted for Hazardous Journey. Small wages, bitter cold, long months of complete darkness, constant danger, safe return doubtful. Honour and recognition in case of success.
>
> —Legendary London advertisement by Shackleton for 1914 expedition into the Antarctic[51]

The Boss picked a diverse group: seamen with various skills (fireman, navigator, engineer, motor expert), doctors, university scientists (physicist, geologist, biologist), carpenter, cook, meteorologist, artist, musician, and photographer. His crew was one of vast harmonious difference, a team of very different temperaments. They ranged all over the map in terms of social class, personalities, and age.

After the initial trip from England to South America, Shackleton discharged a few of the original members of the crew for reasons of bad spirit—including drunkenness—and kicked them off the ship in Buenos Aires. Untested replacements were quickly hired before the team set off for Antarctica.

Shackleton tried never to treat his people as objects or projects. On Shackleton's team, dynamic reciprocities between individuals gave rise to "systems"—that is, the team became more than the aggregate of its individuals and became a system, an organic whole.

Taking Risks

Shackleton was willing to admit his mistakes. At one point he and second-in-command Frank Worsley disagreed about how much ballast should be in the *James Caird*. Later Shackleton admitted that Worsley was right in wanting less ballast.

An expedition is by nature a risk, and every day there were risks. The greatest risk, however, was probably after Shackleton and his men had landed on Elephant Island. Their only hope was South Georgia Island, 800 miles to the east. Cape Horn was only 600 miles away at the tip of South America, but to go due north, across prevailing winds, through Drake's Passage in the winter was a death warrant.

Shackleton was faced with a dilemma. If he left to go for help, it could be said he abandoned his men. If he didn't go for help, it would be said that he played it safe and didn't do all he could do to save them. Shackleton weighed the risks of both choices and made his decision. He left his second-in-command behind and set off with five crewmen in a lifeboat.

At the end of a 17-day, 800-mile journey, Shackleton and the five men with him landed on the south side of

> Here's to the long white road that beckons,
> The climb that baffles, the risk that nerves.
> And here's to the merry heart that reckons
> The rough with the smooth and never swerves.
> —New Zealand school song, one of Shackleton's favorites[52]

South Georgia Island because they feared being washed past the island by winds if they tried to land on the north side, where the settlement was.

After a few days' rest, Shackleton and two of the men headed over a mountain range that had never been crossed. They took no provisions for sleeping, only what they would need to nourish themselves for what they hoped would be a quick journey. Three different dead-end mountain passes made them turn around to find other routes, forcing them to travel in the dark. At the top of the fourth pass, after more than 24 hours of climbing, they looked down into the darkness and couldn't tell if the steeply sloping mountainside ended in a precipice or sloped all the way to the bottom. They didn't have the strength or provisions to look for another route. They couldn't stay there—they would freeze to death. So Shackleton decided to slide down the mountain.

"It's a devil of a risk, but we've got to take it!" Shackleton announced.

"What if we hit a rock?" Crean asked.

"What if the slope doesn't level off?" Worsley wondered aloud.

Shackleton gave the answer in the form of a question: "Can we stay where we are?"[53]

The answer was obvious. Using their coiled ropes as a toboggan, and locking themselves together into a human ball, they bolted down the 4000-foot mountain, dropping a thousand feet a minute, hoping not to hit a rock or kick up an avalanche. Remarkably, they made it down without significant injury.

Crisis doesn't make a person. It reveals you for what you are. You don't know who someone is until adversity comes. It shows the cracks, and the cracks are where God leaks through.

Perhaps the most important survival question the church can ask is, "Can we stay where we are?"

Blessings

Shackleton constantly blessed his crew. His blessings kept them hitting the right notes, notes of hope, camaraderie, and compassion. He kept sounding those notes throughout the long ordeal. Shackleton liberated and empowered his crew by opening up spaces in which they could be creative. He blessed them with his unhectoring spirit. It wasn't a spiritual blessing, but the blessing became spiritual.[54]

Shackleton did everything he could to prevent his men from losing their inner voices. He understood the connection between body and mind and was as concerned about the men's mental and emotional states as their physical condition. You bless people by how you see them and hear them and treat them. His men knew he cared for them.

In 1909, Shackleton had come within 97 miles of the South Pole before Amundsen and Scott. But he turned back from a point known as "Furthest South" (the nearest spot to either pole reached by humans, at that point in time), for which he was roundly criticized. He turned back because he didn't want to risk the lives of his men, for whom he was responsible as their leader. The return itself he called a "race to civilization."

To have a goal so close and then turn around took great courage. The coward's way was to go ahead. The courageous way was to retreat and race home. On that return trip, the small team was rationed bits of food to keep them going. Shackleton gave one of his last biscuits to his colleague, Frank Wild. That is giving a blessing!

Building a Team

Shackleton made sure every little dispute among the *Endurance* crew was resolved as quickly as possible. He made them shake hands and indoctrinated them in the ideology that we sink or swim together. Their only salvation was in solidarity. Although the Cambridge scientists were miles distant from the firemen in their thinking and way of life, no fights broke out among the crew.

The Boss didn't allow gossip or backbiting. Rather than allow conflicts to fester, he created artificial distinctions among his men, making light of things that mattered little—for example, the FAFs versus the FUGs. The Fresh Air Friends were those who wanted to sleep with the hatch open, while the Fetid Under Grounds were those who didn't want to let out the heat.

When camped on the ice and sleeping in close quarters, Shackleton shuffled the men from one tent to another, mixing and matching them to remind them that they were all in this together.

Shackleton was a great believer in maintaining routines. He didn't have ruthlessly enforced rules, but he did ruthlessly enforce routines, which were executed in almost military drill fashion. Like a marching band that finds a oneness in full body-and-soul synchronization, routines were the rhythmic beats that bound bodies and souls together in sonic communion.

Never did Shackleton leave his men without a specific rhythmic regime. Even when they were trapped in the ice floe, he kept the team on a tight schedule. Breakfast at nine; lunch at one; tea at four; dinner at six; and ship's chores in between. He weighed and measured every member of the crew to monitor their weight loss (or gain). They rotated watches regularly, and Shackleton woke the men himself by whistle every morning.

The Boss also created rituals of their journey. While stranded on the ice, on December 5, 1916, he declared a holiday to celebrate the anniversary of their departure from South Georgia Island. At every chance they got, he declared a celebration. When they crossed the Antarctic Circle, they celebrated. When they accomplished something especially difficult, they celebrated. These rituals carried a weight of worship that suggested a form of sanctity in their desperate lives. If all myths are connected to rituals, the Shackleton myth had its origin right here—in team rituals of their trek.[55]

> Anyone can celebrate when something good happens. It's when things go bad that we need to celebrate.
>
> —Guitarist-vocalist Ash DeLorenzo

Why was Shackleton the leader his men needed? Because he created a culture where everyone musicked. No wonder that future explorers said, "When disaster strikes and all hope is gone, get down on your knees and pray for Shackleton."[56]

NOTES

1. This is the common rendering of several lines from Saint Exupéry's poem "Dessine-moi un beateau." A literal translation of the French reads as follows: "To create the ship, / it is not to weave the fabrics, / to forge the nails, / to read the stars, / but to instead give a taste for the sea." See www.spies.com/[~artemis/poitry/dessine-moi.html. Accessed 25 February 2004.
2. With thanks to colleague Craig Hennenfield for this insight.
3. For more on this, see my *SoulTsunami: Sink or Swim in New Millennium Culture* (Grand Rapids: Zondervan, 1999), 178, 300–301, 389–93.
4. See Alan A. Cavaiola and Neil J. Lavender, *Toxic Coworkers: How to Deal with Dysfunctional People on the Job* (Oakland, CA: New Harbinger Publications, 2000), and Barbara Bailey Reinhold, *Toxic Work: How to Overcome Stress, Overload, and Burnout and Revitalize Your Career* (New York: Dutton, 1996).
5. This bridge on the Puget Sound, completed only shortly before its collapse, was considered revolutionary in its design and historic in its catastrophic failure. Its collapse led to new discoveries in aerodynamics and new practices in civil engineering. See *Tacoma Narrows Bridge*, www.nwrain.net/~newtsuit/ recoveries/narrows/narrows.htm. Accessed 28 November 2002.
6. See Stanley Foster Reed, *Toxic Executive* (New York: HarperBusiness, 1992).
7. Three such companies include the New Hope Natural Media of Boulder, Colorado (www.newhope.com), the Benjamin Group/BSMG Worldwide (www.benjamingroup.com), and Plante & Moran (www.plante-moran.com). Accessed 31 May 2003.
8. Midas Dekkers, *The Way of All Flesh: The Romance of Ruins*, trans. Sherry Marx-Macdonald (New York: Farrar, Straus & Giroux, 2000), 251, 250.
9. Political activist/humorist Andrew Boyd in *Daily Afflictions: The Agony of Being Connected to Everything in the Universe* (New York: Norton, 2002), 39.
10. Nadine Stair, "If I Had My Life to Live Over," in *If I Had My Life to Live Over I Would Pick More Daisies*, ed. Sandra Haldeman Martz (Watsonville, CA: Papier-Mache Press, 1992), 1.
11. See Kenneth Lay, "What Should a CEO Expect from a Board?" Presented at University of St. Thomas Center for Business Ethics, Houston, April 1999, entitled "Corporate Governance: Ethics Across the Board," *Corporate Governance Papers*. www.stthom.edu/cbes/conferences/kenneth_lay.html. Accessed 9 May 2003.
12. Barbara Ley Toffler, *Final Accounting: Ambition, Greed, and the Fall of Arthur Andersen* (New York: Broadway Books, 2003).
13. Marianne Moore to Lloyd Frankenberg, December 26, 1943, in *The Selected Letters of Marianne Moore*, ed. Bonnie Costello, Celeste Goodridge, and Cristanne Miller (New York: Alfred A. Knopf, 1997), 443.
14. Quoted in Betsy Bernard, "Seven Golden Rules of Leadership," delivered at the Ninth Annual Business Women's Network Women and Diversity

Leadership Summit, 2002, 8. http://leadership.wharton.upenn.edu/digest/Seven_Golden_Rules.pdf. Accessed 9 May 2003.

15. "Into the Spirit World," *Trend Letter* 18 (4 February 1999), 5–6.

16. Ibid.

17. Jim Collins, *Good to Great: Why Some Companies Make the Leap . . . and Others Don't* (New York: HarperBusiness, 2001), 22.

18. Ibid., 25.

19. Alexander Hamilton, *The Federalist, on the New Constitution, Written in 1788, by Mr. Hamilton, Mr. Madison, and Mr. Jay*, new ed. (Hallowell, ME: Masters, Smith, 1857), 324 (no. 70).

20. Ibid., 328–31 (no. 71). See also "In Regard to the Re-eligibility of the President" (no. 72), 331–35.

21. Ibid., 336 (no. 73).

22. Ibid., 336–40 (no. 73).

23. As quoted in John W. Yates III, "Pottering and Prayer," *Christianity Today* 45 (2 April 2001), 60.

24. The term *risk* comes from the Greek *riza*, which means both root and cliff. For more, see Niels Henrik Gregersen, "Faith in a World of Risks: A Trinitarian Theology of Risk-Taking," in *For All People: Global Theologies in Contexts: Essays in Honor of Viggo Mortensen*, ed. Else Marie Wiberg Pedersen, Holger Lam, and Peter Lodberg (Grand Rapids: Eerdmans, 2002), 216.

25. "Thus antelopes are really indulging in a dangerous waste of energy when they stop in front of a cheetah, but their willingness to risk it is how they tell the cheetah, Don't even bother trying . . . 'you can't touch me'" (Amotz Zahavi's handicap principle as explained in Chetan J. Parikh, "Risky Behavior," Capital Ideas Online, 17 September 2003. www.capitalideasonline.com/chetan/riskybehavior.htm. Accessed 26 December 2003.

26. See James Hillman, *A Blue Fire: Selected Writings* (New York: Harper & Row, 1989), 115.

27. For more, see my "Nerve of Failure," *Theology Today* 34 (1977), 143–49.

28. As cited in Charles Cummings, *Eco-Spirituality: Toward a Reverent Life* (Mahwah, NJ: Paulist Press, 1991), 30.

29. So says Michael Storey, CEO of Immarsat: "People will not be fired for their mistakes, they will be fired only if they don't learn from their mistakes." As quoted in Alison Maitland, "Inside Track: Enthusiast at the Cutting Edge: Under the Skin Michael Storey, INMARSAT," *Financial Times*, 9 October 2000, 12.

30. Michael Marquardt, *Action Learning in Action: Transforming Problems and People for World-Class Organizational Learning* (Palo Alto, CA: Davies-Black Publishing, 1999), 22.

31. "Director of Vibe: Job Titles of the Future: Jennifer Rubell, *Fast Company* (July-August 1999), 56. www.fastcompany.com/online/26/jtrubell.html. Accessed 29 November 2002.

32. See William H. McNeill, *Keeping Together in Time: Dance and Drill in Human History* (Cambridge, MA: Harvard University Press, 1995), esp. the conclusion, 151–57.

33. Stanford W. Gregory and Stephen Webster, "A Nonverbal Signal in Voices of Interview Partners Effectively Predict Communication Accommodation and

Social Status Perceptions," *Journal of Personality and Social Psychology* 70 (1996), 1,234.

34. As cited in Richad Conniff, *The Natural History of the Rich: A Field Guide* (New York: W. W. Norton, 2003), 76–77.
35. William L. Benzon, *Beethoven's Anvil: Music in Mind and Culture* (New York: Basic Books, 2001), 89.
36. Ibid., 88.
37. For more on the American Music Therapy Association, see www.musictherapy.org. Accessed 11 May 2003.
38. Dennis O'Rourke, quoting Les Murray as quoted in Neil James, "How the Poet Got His Wounds," *TLS: Times Literary Supplement* (5 January 2001), 6.
39. Mark Sanborn, "The Holographic Team and the Code for Success," #145 from *R&D Innovator* 4, no. 3 (March 1995). www.winstonbrill.com/bril001/html/article_index/articles/101-150/article145_body.html. Accessed 28 May 2003.
40. Ronald Stuart Thomas, "The Tree," in his *Collected Poems 1945–1990* (London: Phoenix Giant, 1995), 417.
41. With appreciation to Mark Ernsberger (president and CEO of Farr Associates), "Leadership: It Is Not for the Faint of Heart," *Vital Speeches of the Day* 66 (1 June 2000), 511.
42. Frederick B. Burnham, "Cops and Burgers: Seeing Order In Chaos—and Vise Versa," *Spirituality & Health* (Fall 2002). www.spiritualityhealth.com/newsh/items/article/item_5349.html. Accessed 11 May 2003.
43. See Peter Koestenbaum's interview with Polly LaBarre, "Do You Have the Will to Lead?" *Fast Company* (March 2000), 230. www.fastcompany.com/online/32/koestenbaum.html. Accessed 26 December 2002.
44. Robert Musil, *The Man without Qualities*, trans. Eithne Wilkins and Ernst Kaiser (New York: Secker & Warburg, 1953), 1:243.
45. Thomas R. Hawkins, *Faithful Leadership: Learning to Lead with Power* (Nashville: Discipleship Resources, 1999), 102.
46. "When Companies Connect," *Economist* (24 June 1999), 19.
47. Cheryl Russell, "The New Consumer Paradigm," *American Demographics* (April 1999), 58.
48. Paul Taylor, "How the Internet Will Reshape Worldwide Business Activity," in "Survey: Information Technology section," *Financial Times* (7 April 1999), I.
49. Caroline Alexander, *The Endurance: Shackleton's Legendary Antarctic Expedition* (New York: Alfred A. Knopf, 1998), 54.
50. Apocryphal notice as quoted in Kim Heacox, *Shackleton: The Antarctic Challenge* (Washington, DC: National Geographic, 1999), 34.
51. Alfred Lansing, *Endurance* (New York: Carroll & Graf, 2001), 13.
52. Quoted in Jennifer Armstrong, *Shipwreck at the Bottom of the World: The Extraordinary True Story of Shackleton and the Endurance* (New York: Crown, 1998), 126.
53. Quoted in ibid., 111.
54. For more on this, see David Spangler, *Blessing: The Art and the Practice* (New York: Riverhead Books, 2001), 127–30.
55. For the operational relationships of myth and ritual, see Robert A. Segal, ed., *The Myth and Ritual Theory* (Malden, MA: Blackwell, 1998).
56. Quoted in Dennis N. T. Perkins, *Leading at the Edge: Leadership Lessons from the Extraordinary Saga of Shackleton's Antarctic Expedition* (New York: AMACOM, 2000), 10.

Surround Sound

*A Song for Everyone
to Sing*

> A machine has a sole purpose; a human organization
> has a *soul* purpose. The soul purpose is not about
> money; it's about actualizing dreams of a higher pur-
> pose that serve the greatest good.
>
> —Roger Lewin and Birute Regine[1]

In the not-too-distant past, growth was all that mattered in corporate America—that and a successful Arthur Andersen audit.

But there's a different measure today. The question is, What
is real growth? Not numerical growth, but authentic growth.
Growth is not a mission; service and human betterment are
missions. In the words of the foremost corporate consultant in
Europe, Charles Handy:

> I once sat up on stage with a C.E.O. in front of the senior
> members of his company. The C.E.O. said his goal was to cre-
> ate the world's largest organization. He wanted to grow at a
> truly astronomical rate. I said to him that the two largest
> organizations in the world today are the Red Army in China
> and the British National Health Service. And I asked him
> whether either of those two models was what he had in
> mind. He was rather embarrassed. Suddenly, growth for its
> own sake seemed to be a very funny notion.[2]

Mission can no longer be the old understandings of
"growth." Growth-oriented companies are now treated with

more than a measure of suspicion; a growth obsession is now seen as a liability, not an asset. Past hunger for growth and hunger for acquisitions led to aggressive accounting, and that's what got Enron and others in trouble.

Leonard E. Read, founder of the think tank Foundation for Economic Education in Irvington, New York, in 1945, tells of a shopper in a crowded department store during a Christmas rush. After buying some gifts, she remarks to a clerk on how jammed the store is. "Yes," says the clerk, "it's our best day so far." Then the shopper goes over to the post office to mail her packages, again remarking on the crowd. "Yes," says a postal clerk, "it's our worst day so far."[3]

These two clerks were on very different missions. We need to be sure we're on the right one. Too many times church leaders pat themselves on the back for the kind of growth that becomes "the worst day so far."

A LEADER'S MISSION

The church has always been about mission, but it might be instructive to look at the concept of mission as seen through the eyes of corporate leadership. Nearly every company these days has a mission statement, partly because corporate leaders understand the value of helping people connect with something much bigger than themselves—even bigger than their company.

There is a mission to life. There is a mission for every person. God has a mission for our lives. And it has to be bigger than ourselves—certainly bigger than "growth." A life of mission is the mission of life.

The opportunity for mission is great because the problems are huge. No one person, corporation, or organization can solve them alone. Across the world, 1.3 billion people live on less than $1 a day; 3 billion people live on under $2 a day; 1.3 billion have no access to clean water; 3 billion have no access to sanitation; 2 billion have no access to electrical power. When it comes to missions bigger than ourselves, there are plenty to go around!

A mission is what buys us life space. To be born is to be chosen—chosen for a mission. If you're alive, your mission on earth is unfinished.

A leader's mission is to enlist people in a mission they care about—one that will change history, go down in history—and then get the mission going. Everyone is searching for a "higher purpose." Everyone wants to be part of a mission that they care about, a mission that will change the world. Mission is what gets people motivated.

I find that one needs some *really* pure single activity.

—Novelist D. H. Lawrence[4]

Leaders are driven by a passionate inner music and help others find the passion of the music that beats inside them. Leaders give everyone a mission. People will work for a company and give blood, sweat, and tears for a mission. People will put in time for a job; they will give their lives for a mission.

Some companies already get it, as seen in their advertising:

- Southwest Airlines isn't in the air travel business—it's in the "Freedom" business.
- Fannie Mae isn't in the mortgage-lending business—it's in the "American Dream" business.
- The Air Force isn't in the military business—it's in the "winning" business.

What mission are you in?

"Mission control" is an oxymoron. We can't control missions. Circumstances will change. Plans will fail. Instead of planning our missions, we must compose them without plans. We must schedule in the serendipity and improvisation.

We have already stated that leadership is a dance, but every encounter with another person is a dance. Part of interpersonal relationships is learning the different steps and rhythms of people. When two people feel each other's beat, they learn when to lead, when to follow, and when to stand there and enjoy the music. A mature soul has learned to read the energy fields of others. Some people give off low vibrations; others are high-wattage. Some people suck energy out of you; others plug you into the energies of the universe.

> Physicists and philosophers won't know anything until they learn to dance.
>
> —Friedrich Nietzsche[5]

A leader helps people find their song and sing their song. A leader helps others hear the cosmic fugue. A leader helps people move from living their lives to *singing* their lives. A leader helps them realize that they are part of a score larger than themselves—not "God has a plan for you," but "you are part of God's larger purposes and design."

Everyone has a story to tell, a secret to impart, a song to sing. A leader's job is to find the melody line around which everyone can harmonize.

The song can save the world. Songs convey and purvey hope. They're worth leaving the boat for. Be willing to sacrifice for the song.

I remember a sweet fable from first grade. A group of old monks could not sing very well, but croaked on in their prayers of the hours (I didn't know that term in first grade!). One day a young monk joined them. When it came to prayer time, the young man sang so beautifully that all of the monks stopped their singing to listen, dazzled by him. This went on for months until finally an angel came to the abbot. "Why have you stopped praying?" asked the angel. "God no longer hears your prayers. Why?" The abbot explained about the new monk whose voice rivaled the voices of the angels. The angel shook his head and explained how important the prayers were to God and how he looked forward to hearing from them each evening. The young monk with the beautiful voice had to leave so that the old monks could be heard by God.

It has always been for me a story that spoke volumes: Not stay where you are, but recognize how God is calling you in your midst. How God wants to hear your song.

The world is too vast for every thing and every one to be on the same wavelength. We need harmony between wavelengths—between the experimental and the experiential—not hegemony of one wavelength over another. A constant harping on a single string, no matter how sweet the tone, becomes a bore.

All great leaders tell stories or embody stories that resonate with others. Mission needs to be related in narrative form. Narrative flair and rhetorical prowess go a long way in persuading people to join the mission.

Great leaders also invite participation. The cards of leadership are not held close to the chest. Leaders invite feedback. And they listen! "He doesn't listen" is one of the greatest possible condemnations of a leader. The leader must listen as a conductor does and conduct according to what he hears. We can no longer afford to expect *thinking* to be a function of those at the top and *doing* to be a function of those at the bottom. None of us is as smart as all of us. The mission depends on everyone.

Participation increases the power of the leader rather than diminishing it: Montesquieu (1689–1755) is famous for his principle of the *Trias Politica*, the foundation of

> I don't think I've chosen this life; I feel I've been pushed into it. And what sustains me is a sense of my life as a mission.
> —Scientist Jane Goodall[6]

the US Constitution. He pointed out that separated and distributed power meant "freedom." The inverse—power concentrated in one hand—meant that "All was lost."[7]

Make Waves

In the past, every "job"—all physical labor—was a religious activity, a sacred exertion. *Laborare est orare* is the way the monks used to put it: "To labor is to pray, work is worship." We've separated our work from the spiritual realm, but it's an artificial distinction. Make your work your mission; your work can be your spiritual practice.

Turn every job into a mission.

Some people make big splashes (one-shot affairs); others make waves. Waves carry the vibration on and on and on. Be a wave-maker. Help people find a shared motivation. Then the mission will succeed—partly because other surfers show up where the big waves are rushing. Surfers don't go to the beach and wait for the waves; they go where the waves are already crashing.[8]

Just as the more global our world gets, the more tribal it becomes, so the more decentralized and pluralistic and fragmented the world is getting, the more it needs to call forth leaders who can help people unite behind shared dreams. In the future, everyone will get more than 15

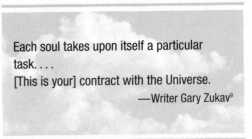

Each soul takes upon itself a particular task. . . .
[This is your] contract with the Universe.
—Writer Gary Zukav[9]

minutes of fame, as Andy Warhol promised. Everyone will get 15 minutes to save the world. The world can't survive without these leaders.[10]

Character does not exist to exist; it only comes into its own when it is enlisted in the cause of a mission. It is a moral imperative of leadership to give yourself to something larger than yourself. Joy comes not because we work for it or aim for it in life; joy comes our way while we're on a mission larger than we are.

A "singularity" is something that cannot be explained or duplicated. A mission is a singularity; everything in life comes into focus when one is "on mission."

What we're describing here is what William W. George, chair and CEO of Medtronics, calls "leadership with purpose," which he defines as "leadership with vision, with passion, and with compassion."[11]

> Transcendent leadership of an organization, as I see it, envisions a clear mission for the organization, a mission with purpose and passion, and calls upon that purpose and that passion to lead the organization to greater heights to fulfill its mission.[12]

According to George, a leadership mission gives everyone involved with a company a reason to be devoted to it, including customers and stakeholders. It provides a purpose, beyond what can be described in terms of finances. In the end, what counts is not how much money we made, but how we treated other people.[13] James W. Rouse, founder of the commercial development Rouse Company, is famous for saying, "Profit is not the legitimate purpose of business. Its purpose is to provide a service needed by society. If this is done efficiently, companies will be profitable."[14]

The idea of mission is definitely catching on in marketing. Have you seen the Shell ad that features a smoky sky obstructing the Shell logo and a blue sky with a clear logo? Bridging the two is this: 'Profits & Principles: Is there a Choice?" The text reads, "The issue of global warming has given rise to heated debate. Is the burning of fossil fuels and increased concentration of carbon dioxide in the air a serious threat or just a lot of hot air?"

Shell answers its own ad:

> Shell believes that action needs to be taken now, both by companies and their customers. So last year, we renewed our commitment not only to meet the agreed Kyoto targets to reduce greenhouse gas emissions, but to exceed them. We're working to increase the provision of cleaner burning natural gas and encouraging the use of lower-carbon fuels for homes and transport. It's all part of our commitment to sustainable development, balancing economic progress with environmental care and social responsibility."[15]

According to some polls, with no difference in price or quality, 76 percent of consumers would switch brands if in so doing they would support a cause. In another poll, 75 percent of graduating MBA students said that a company should factor into its profit considerations issues of environment, community involvement, family strengthening, etc. Fifty percent of these MBA grads said they would take a cut in salary to work for a socially responsible company.[16]

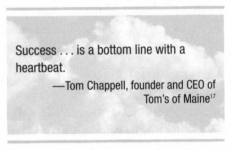

Success . . . is a bottom line with a heartbeat.
—Tom Chappell, founder and CEO of Tom's of Maine[17]

Spirituality and Mission

It may seem ironic to look to the business world for spiritual enlightenment, but the new emphasis on spirituality in the marketplace ought to be an encouragement for church leaders. After all, isn't that our specialty? Spirituality is once again taking its place in our world after the modernist swap of spirituality for rationality.

In Europe, spirituality is often a more highly accepted part of healing than in USAmerica. In some clinics there, the doctor says to a person with cancer, "You have cancer. Do you want me to heal you, or do you want me to help you complete the circle of your life?" If the patient opts for healing, then the doctor says, "Then you must tell me your mission. Why is it that you must live? Specifically, what must you accomplish?"

The first step in their treatment is the establishment of mission.[18]

Spiritual values are also showing up in the business world: Growing numbers of companies are openly managing from a more spiritual point of view.[19]

William E. Simon, Jr., Executive Director of William E. Simon & Sons in LA, states: "Until recently I viewed business as an activity that generated income and intellectual stimulation." Now, he says, business "may be pursued with God's will in mind and indeed should be pursued in that manner."[20]

Architect Frank Gehry claims to be more and more aware of "the presence of a great power that is holding it all together."[21] He sees architecture as a means of helping others: "It is some kind of medium that I have been blessed with and I look at it as the work of making the best use of it for the help of others."[22]

As the business world sees the leader's role as rearranging reality and filtering facts into iconic symbols of healing and redemption, how much more should the church be very clear about it's mission of healing and redemption.

Shackleton was lost when he was without a mission. Another person like that was Alexander Hamilton, who ranks under Washington with the pantheon of Adams, Jefferson, and Madison. After he retired from political office, Hamilton wandered about as a lost soul. In fact,

> They respected that I came in with a mission.
> Richard Hatch, winner of first *Survivor*[23]

one recent biographer (Richard Brookhiser) suggests that he entered the famous duel with Aaron Burr as an act of public service. Brookhiser suggests that Hamilton knew Burr would aim to kill while he intended to aim wide and high himself, thereby sacrificing his life so that a person he deemed a cancer on the body politic would be forever discredited.[24]

You are here with a mission. God is guiding you every day in your mission. Sing your song and help others sing theirs.

| SHACKLETON MODULATIONS: | A Bold Mission • Survival |

When Ernest Shackleton was not on a mission, he could not make a right decision. He messed up his personal life, his finances, his career, and almost everything he touched when he was not on a mission. It seemed that in day to day living his life was one missed boat after another, whether coming or going.

But when he was "on mission," he almost could not make a wrong decision. Like Lord Nelson, he was "godlike at sea but on land he was adrift."

Shackleton was no dummy. He realized what others eventually saw: when he wasn't on a mission he was worthless. Like a spinning top that you have to keep slapping or it topples over, once Shackleton stopped being slapped in shape by a mission, he collapsed. He confessed to his wife, Emily, "I am just good as an explorer and nothing else."[25] This confession was echoed by his arch rival Robert Scott in a final letter to his wife, Kathleen, from the South Pole. "I wasn't a very good husband," Scott penned in a shaky hand, "but I hope I shall be a good memory."[26]

A Bold Mission

Ernest Shackleton's *Endurance* expedition stands as one of the biggest challenges in maritime history. The intended mission was big enough: to cross the 1,800-mile wide, frozen and barren Antarctic continent from the Weddell Sea to the Ross Sea via the South Pole–"the last great Antarctic adventure."

Had all gone as intended, the mission would have been a dramatic survival story. As it was, the story is beyond dramatic.

Sometimes missions change. Shackleton's mission changed first when ice chewed up the ship. Shackleton and his men were stranded on drifting ice, 2000 miles from the tip of South America. The morning after they took up residence on the ice, Shackleton wrote in his diary: "Though we have been compelled to abandon the ship, which is crushed beyond all hope of ever being righted, we are alive and well, and we have stores and equipment for the task that lies before us. The task is to reach land with all the members of the expedition."[27]

The Boss announced their new mission and strategy: they would walk across the frozen sea, hauling two of the three lifeboats to Paulet Island, 346 miles to the northwest. Shackleton knew that on Paulet Island stood some abandoned huts from a 1902 Swedish expedition. He didn't tell anyone of a plan to proceed from there. He would figure that out later. What they needed at the time was hope for the future, a mission more than a blueprint.

The trip would be the equivalent of walking across Iowa hauling two one-ton-each lifeboats, plus gear. And this Iowa was treacherous Antarctic ice. But they had a mission.

Each crew member was given a two-pound limit on personal gear–excluding diaries and tobacco. In a dramatic symbolic gesture, Shackleton pulled out his gold cigarette case, dug all the gold coins from his pocket, and dropped them on the snow. These were not necessary for survival.[28] Then he tore the fly-leaf out of the Bible that Queen Alexandra had given to the ship—with her own writing on it—and also the wonderful page of Job containing the verse:

Out of whose womb came the ice?

And the hoary frost of Heaven, who hath gendered it?

The waters are hid as with a stone,

And the face of the deep is frozen.[29]

He then folded this page, put it in his pocket, and placed the heavy Bible on top of the gold coins and case. Time now to travel light. However, once again, Shackleton ordered Hussey to keep his banjo.

After two days of backbreaking drudgery, dragging the boats across the rough ice floes, they had advanced less than two miles from the crushed ship. After serious contemplation, Shackleton announced a different strategy: they would set up camp on the ice and wait for the drifting ice to take them northward. He also sent men back to retrieve whatever they could from what they had abandoned two days earlier. They saved more than three tons of food, the third lifeboat, and 150 out of the 400 precious glass photographic plates Frank Hurley had saved.[30]

Survival

Now the new mission began: survive months of waiting. Shackleton knew his men needed things to do, so he kept a strict routine, assigned jobs to everyone, and made sure each man did his part.

As the journey continued, the mission had to change again and again because the uncontrollable circumstances around them changed. But whatever happened, they always had a mission. You can't control what happens to you. You can only control how you respond to it. Through regular conversations with every crew member, The Boss kept his finger on the pulse of his crew. He knew when a man needed encouragement, and when another needed a kick in the posterior.

When spirits seemed lowest, he always came up with something—sometimes as simple as games on the ice or an extra portion of food—to keep the men going. There was never any violence, or even serious conflict. He kept each man singing his own song, in harmony with the rest of the choir. Without a mission, Shackleton may have been worthless. But with a mission, he accomplished what few would have thought possible: He led all his men to safety—not one was lost!

NOTES

1. Roger Lewin and Birute Regine, *The Soul at Work: Embracing Complexity Science for Business Success* (New York: Simon & Schuster, 2000), 325.
2. Charles Handy, as quoted in Joel Kurtzman, "An Interview with Charles Handy," *Strategy & Business: The CEO Survival Kit* 1 (1998), 19. Online version, *Strategy+Business*, 4th quarter 1995, 5. www.strategy-business.com/thoughtleaders/95405/. Accessed 30 August 2001.
3. As quoted in William H. Peterson, "Free Trade and Capitalism: America's Other Democracy," *Vital Speeches of the Day* 65 (1 April 1999), 375.
4. D. H. Lawrence, *Women in Love* (New York: Viking Press, 1970), 50.
5. As quoted in William L. Benzon, *Beethoven's Anvil: Music in Mind and Culture* (New York: Basic Books, 2001), 47.
6. As quoted in "Media Diet: Jane Goodall," as interviewed by Karen Olson, *Utne Reader* (September-October 2000), 113.
7. Arie de Geus, *The Living Company* (Boston: Harvard Business School Press, 1997), 198.
8. With thanks to Hugo Gygax Rodriguez of Green Lake, Wisconsin, for this metaphor.
9. "Each soul takes upon itself a particular task. . . . Whatever the task that your soul has agreed to, whatever its contract with the Universe, all the experiences of your life serve to awaken within you the memory of that contract, and to prepare you to fulfill it." See Gary Zukav, *The Seat of the Soul* (New York: Simon & Schuster, 1989), 335–36.
10. See the comments of John W. Gardner on "Leadership and Power" in *Leadership Papers* 4 (Washington, DC: Independent Sector), (October 1986), 19: "There are systems that can survive for considerable periods without leadership, but our pluralistic society is not one of them," as referenced in Sam Portaro and Gary Peluso, *Inquiring and Discerning Hearts: Vocation and Ministry with Young Adults on Campus* (Atlanta: Scholars Press, 1993), 259.
11. William W. George, "Leadership: Building a Mission-Driven, Values-Centered Organization," *Vital Speeches of the Day* 65 (1 May 1999), 440.
12. Ibid.
13. Ibid., 441.
14. As quoted in Dominic A. Tarantino, "At a Crossroads: The Global Community, Global Business and the Caux Round Table: Presented to The Keidanren Subcommittee on the Charter for Good Corporate Behavior, 4 March 1998." www.cauxroundtable.org/Sp_TP1.HTM. Accessed 31 January 2002.

15. The ad appeared in *Financial Times* (14 November 2000). See also Kenny Bruno, "Shell: Clouding the Issue: Special to CorpWatch," *CorpWatch* (15 November 2000). www.corpwatch.org/campaigns/PCD.jsp?articleid=218. Accessed 31 December 2002.
16. David Dorsey, "The New Spirit at Work," *Fast Company* 16 (August 1998), 124. www.fastcompany.com/online/16/barrett.html. Accessed 4 April 2003.
17. As quoted in Anna Muoio, "The Secrets of Their Success—and Yours: Unit of One," *Fast Company* (June-July 1997), 67. www.fastcompany.com/magazine/09/one.html. Accessed 4 April 2003.
18. With thanks to email from Tim Forbess, Tforbess@aol.com, 18 March 1999.
19. See Laura Nash, *Church on Sunday, Work on Monday: The Challenge of Fusing Christian Values with Business Life* (San Francisco: Jossey-Bass, 2001). Few have gone as far as the British retailer Laura Ashley, which added evangelist Pat Robertson for a time as a non-executive director. See Gordon Bowness, "Heavenly Prints, Fashion/Pat Robertson Fashion Tips," 25 February 1999. www.xtra.ca/site/toronto2/arch/body119.shtm. See also C. Barillas, "Robertson Forced from Laura Ashley Board," *The Data Lounge* (9 June 1999). www.datalounge.com/datalounge/news/record.html?record=4337.
20. As quoted in Donald P. Merrifield, S.J., "Beyond Good and Evil: A Worldly Spirituality," *Vital Speeches of the Day* 65 (15 March 1999), 340.
21. Ibid., 339.
22. Ibid., 340.
23. Quoted by Gary Levin, "The 'Survivor' Tribe Has Spoken: It's Richard," *USA Today*, 24 August 2000, 1D.
24. Richard Brookhiser, *Alexander Hamilton, American* (New York: Free Press, 1999), 210–11.
25. Jennifer Armstrong, *Shipwreck at the Bottom of the World: The Extraordinary True Story of Shackleton and the Endurance* (New York: Crown, 1998), 5.
26. As quoted in Peter Brent, *Captain Scott and the Antarctic Tragedy* (London: Weidenfeld & Nicolson, 1974), 202.
27. Armstrong, *Shipwreck at the Bottom of the World*, 50–51.
28. Ibid., 51.
29. Job 38:29–30 KJV, quoted in Ernest Shackleton, *South: The Story of Shackleton's 1914–1917 Expedition* (London: Heinemann, 1970), 35.
30. Armstrong, *Shipwreck at the Bottom of the World*, 53–54.

What Big Ears You Have!

Sound Checks and Sounding Boards

> The heart of the discerning acquires knowledge; the ears of the wise seek it out.
>
> —Proverbs 18:15 NIV

Poet Robert Frost had a theory of poetic voice he called "the sound of sense." Frost contended that he actually heard voices, from nowhere and everywhere, that gave to him his poems.[1]

The world is alive with sounds that we often attribute to the voice of God. Might his thundering voice be present in all the sounds we hear, yet it falls on deaf ears because we have not been accustomed to listen broadly?

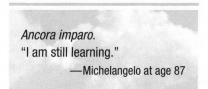

Ancora imparo.
"I am still learning."
—Michelangelo at age 87

We need to open our ears and listen to the sounding boards around us. Acoustic competence assumes a lifetime of constant listening and learning.

BECOMING A LEARNER

"May you live in interesting times."

Robert Kennedy liked to use this quote in his speeches in the 1960s. He called it an ancient Chinese curse.

The truth is, Kennedy didn't get it from the Chinese. It came from a British science fiction writer, Eric Frank Russell (pen name Duncan H. Monro).[2]

The truth is, it's not ancient. Unless the 1950s are ancient. The truth is, it's not a curse. It's a blessing. We may yearn for *less* interesting times, but these are the times in which we have been called and chosen to lead.

To be open to the future—to be open to these "interesting times"—is to be open to what you don't know. A biblical proverb says, "The fear of the LORD is the beginning of wisdom."[3] Wisdom is a journey, a path, a lifelong pilgrimage, a path of many steps and stops, sunrises and sunsets.

What you don't know *can* hurt you. Ask Enron, Andersen, Global Crossing, Merrill Lynch, Tyco, ImClone, the FBI, the CIA, or the Catholic Church.

A look at the disastrous events of 9/11 clearly demonstrates the consequences of our inability to deal responsibly and effectively with information.

How much can happen in one lifetime? People are still alive today who began life when there were "no vitamin tablets, no antibiotics, no television, no dial telephones, no refrigerators, no FM radio, no synthetic fibers, no dishwashers, no electric blankets, no airmail, no transatlantic airlines, no instant coffee, no Xerox, no air-conditioning, no frozen foods, no contact lenses, no birth control pills, no ball-point pens, no transistors."[4]

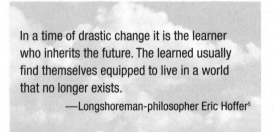

In a time of drastic change it is the learner who inherits the future. The learned usually find themselves equipped to live in a world that no longer exists.

—Longshoreman-philosopher Eric Hoffer[5]

SKULLS AND EARS

I used to be a learned Professor.

I no longer profess to be a learned Professor. I'm now a learner.

Academic institutions can be citadels of learnedness without being citadels of learning. I recently received a solicitation from my alma mater that describes the school in dramatic terms: "preparing ministers who are pastoral, prophetic, and learned."

That's the problem. We've become "learned." We think we've learned all we need to. That's why God has often set the learned on their ears, even "hiding these things from the learned and the clever and revealing them to little children."[6]

I saw a former student of mine recently and introduced him to someone: "Here's _____. He and I studied together in the early 1990s." I wouldn't have said it that way a few years ago. But faculty need to be students, and vice versa. We "study together" or we stay apart. In a world that everywhere creates "killing fields," we need to create "knowledge fields"—or better yet, learning fields.

People can be divided into two groups: the learned and the learners. The learned I call "skulls." At a certain point early in life, the skull gets as big as it's going to get. The skull freezes in the form it's in for the rest of its life.

The learners I call "ears." Your ears keep growing until the day you die. The difference between skulls people and ears people is that skulls have closed their minds and fused them shut, while ears keep asking new questions and are not afraid to face new challenges.

The Bible's favorite Greek word for a follower of Jesus is *mathetes*. We translate it 269 times as "disciple," but it can equally well be translated as "learner." In the New Testament, love of Jesus and love of learning were strands of a single cloth.

The 21st century needs ears. Nine months after the century was birthed, its first child was born: 11 September 2001. Nine-Eleven has been called a massive "failure of intelligence," or as *Newsweek* corrected it, a failure of imagination (did anyone even imagine its possibility?). The failure of our "intelligence" agencies created a security crisis that resulted in the deaths of thousands of people from more than 60 countries. (Note that the skullish name of one agency—Central Intelligence Agency, or CIA—reveals part of the problem: only *decentralized* intelligence can win "netwars.")

But that failure tells only a small story in a much larger drama. There is a whole new world out there. And if we are not all to literally become skulls, the learned must become learners.

> Real ethics is about remaining open to the Other, which also means remaining open to the future, which means remaining open to what you don't know.
>
> —Researcher Michael Fortun of Rensselaer Polytechnic Institute[7]

The first step in becoming an ear is to admit that what used to work no longer does.

Air Force General Richard Myers, who became chairman of the U.S. Joint Chiefs of Staff in October 2001, admits to being trained and educated "for a different war than we're in."[8] President George W. Bush confesses our need to "come to terms with the new realities of our world."[9]

What should be our responses to these "intelligence failures"? We can rail against leaders who have let us down by not coming to terms with these new realities. We can lament our decades-long vulnerability to attack caused by leaders who have spent hundreds of billions of dollars a year preparing us for everything but the real world and the real dangers we face.

Or we can grow ears.

The government's colossal failure to ensure our safety as citizens is matched only by the church's failure to gird and guard their members in patterns of discipleship that will help them to faithfully follow their Teacher into this new world. We lack intelligence in more ways than one. Have you ever experienced "gridlock" on the highway? Mental and spiritual gridlock can be even more difficult to get out of than physical gridlock.

The world needs more ears. Even the "learned" must admit that we can't comprehend it all. Every course I "teach" is an exercise in intelligence gathering. It gets me out of my gridlocked state by showing me how the life of the mind is a life of learning.

LEARNING A LIVING

My kids expect change and count on fluidity the way I used to expect stability and fixity. Guess who's not going to be disappointed? Their expectations are more in keeping with the truth of the organic world. Change is constant and systematic.

Marvin, the junior trader in the 1986 movie *Wall Street*, shouts into the phone, "I need the information now. In ten minutes I'm history. At four o'clock I'm a dinosaur!" And he's not exaggerating.

> He who learns but does not think is lost. He who thinks but does not learn is in great danger.
>
> —Confucius

I used to work for Coleco in Mayfield, New York. In 1985 Cabbage Patch Kids dominated the market. People wanting the dolls, which were in short supply, created riots in stores. After that blockbuster year, Coleco kept producing Cabbage Patch Kids, but didn't introduce anything new.

Coleco went bankrupt in 1988.

Here's how fast things move: In a matter of two weeks, a 90-year-old firm named Arthur Andersen, which had thousands of employees and billions of dollars of goodwill, was practically destroyed by one word: Enron.

The more we know, the more we know how much there is to know and how little we really know. The more our knowledge of the universe expands, the more we know the universe itself is expanding and the more there is to know.

To store a gigabyte's worth of data 20 years ago required a refrigerator-sized machine weighing 500 pounds. Today that same gigabyte of data lives on a disc smaller than a quarter. The speed, capacity, and performance of technologies have exploded. They have increased by six orders of magnitude over the past 30 years. That's 10 times 10 . . . six times.

Forget megabytes, gigabytes, and nanoseconds. Instead, think "yotta bytes" and "yocto seconds." In ten years we will be measuring memory capacity in terms of "yotta bytes"—10 to the 24th power, or a million-trillion megabytes of information. And we will be measuring processor clock speeds in terms of "yocto seconds"—10 to the minus-24th power.

Consider the GNR revolution (genetic engineering, nanotechnology, robotics). We are building machines today that are measured in nanometers. A nanometer is to an inch what an inch is to 400 miles.

Telephone connections are increasing exponentially as well. Half as many landlines were laid in the last six years of the 20th century as in the whole previous history of the world. From 1995 to 2001, landlines for telephones in China alone soared from 41 million to 179 million. And it's not news to anyone that mobile telephony witnessed even greater growth. The number of active cell phones in the world grew tenfold during those same six years from 91 million to 946 million. Senegal went from 100 mobile phone subscribers to 390,800. Egypt went from 7,400 to almost 3 million.[10]

More information has been collected in the past three years than had been collected before that since the

> The illiterate of the 21st century will not be those who cannot read and write, but those who cannot learn, unlearn, and relearn.
>
> —Futurist Alvin Toffler

beginning of time.[11] More than 100,000 scientific journals annually publish new research from the world's laboratories. But the distance between the amount of information being generated and our ability to alchemize that information into knowledge and wisdom is growing ever greater

We need to learn how to *forget* what we know. In 1997 my son obtained a Ph.D. in biology, toxicology, and immunology. With the half-life of a scientific education being six years, I like to tell him that his Ph.D. is now about as useful as my appendix.

Since I have moved from being learned to a learner, here's how I'm learning a living:

1. When I was learned, life was a quiz show. Now that I'm a learner, life is a Discovery Channel.

2. When I was learned, it was a question of how much I knew. Now that I'm a learner, it's a question of how much I'm being stretched.

3. When I was learned, knowledge was everything. Now that I'm a learner, kindness is everything.

4. When I was learned, knowledge went to my head. Now that I'm a learner, knowledge travels the longest foot in the universe—the foot that separates my head from my heart.

5. When I was learned, I used to point my finger and pontificate. Now that I'm a learner, I slap my forehead all the time.

6. When I was learned, I used to think I was the best. Now that I'm a learner, I do the best I can.

7. When I was learned, I was frightened of new ideas. Now that I'm a learner, I'm even more frightened of *old* ideas.

8. When I was learned, I looked to the past—to have confirmed the set of beliefs I already had. Now that I'm a learner, I look to the future—to grow, be stretched, and remain open to what I don't know.

9. When I was learned, I knew where I was going. Now that I'm a learner, I don't know where I'm going—but I know whom I'm going with.

10. When I was learned, I loved to talk. Now that I'm a learner, I'm slow to speak and quick to listen.

11. When I was learned, I had something to teach everybody. Now that I'm a learner, everybody has something to teach me.

12. When I was learned, I was impatient with dumb people. Now that I'm a learner, I'm grateful when people are patient enough to dumb down to me and care enough to smarten me up.

13. When I was learned, I thought all knowledge was a form of power. Now that I'm a learner, I suspect much knowledge is a form of weakness.

14. When I was learned, I knew where my nose was headed. Now that I'm a learner, I go where my nose leads me.

15. When I was learned, my life revolved around what other people thought about me. Now that I'm a learner, my life revolves around what I think about myself and what God thinks about me.

16. When I was learned, from the high ground of hindsight I instructed the past on where it went wrong. Now that I'm a learner, the past instructs me about how I can right the future.

17. When I was learned, the power and mystery were in the big words. Now that I'm a learner, the power and mystery are in the small, simple words.

18. When I was learned, I thought the educational system was so much better than the market, the other main channel for the mediation of cultural capital. Now that I'm a learner, I realize just how closed and controlling the knowledge industry can be.

19. When I was learned, I deemed the great threats those made dangerous by strength. Now that I'm a learner, I deem the great threats those made dangerous by weakness.
20. When I was learned, I loved to fill out questionnaires. Now that I'm a learner, questionnaires are an exercise in saying "I dunno," since I keep checking the "don't know" box. ("Don't know" doesn't mean "don't care.")
21. When I was learned, I was always trying to speed things up. Now that I'm a learner, I'm always trying to slow things down, even when I'm speeding up.
22. When I was learned, I bragged about how our knowledge is an ever-deepening ocean. Now that I'm a learner, I shudder at how our wisdom is an ever-shrinking drop.
23. When I was learned, I said, "Take it from me." Now that I'm a learner, I say, "Don't take it from me." I boast no immaculate perceptions. I see through a glass *dimly*.

The church needs leaders who are learners, not learned. How would your leadership change if you made that transition?

But I am an academic. One of my images of heaven is a library.[12] And I've seen the movie *My Big Fat Greek Wedding*. So I have a bottle of Windex and am cleaning that glass for all it's worth. I'm trying to get rid of as much fog and film as I can. But the best I will ever do is to "know in part." I will never "know it all." God's ways are not our ways.[13] Only on the other side will that darkened glass be transformed into a perfect prism. Only then shall I see "face to face" and "know even as I am known."

Again: Don't take it from me. Don't believe everything I say just because I said it. Remember, I'm a learner, not learned. "Seldom, very seldon," says the narrator of Jane Austen's *Emma*, "does complete truth belong to any human disclosure; seldom can it happen that something is not a little disguised, or a little mistaken."[14]

I warn my students that at my very best, 80 percent of my theology is correct, 20 percent is wrong. The problem is, I'm not sure which is the 80 percent and which isn't.

You don't think heaven is going to be a seminary education? You don't think eternity is going to require some theological adjustments?

You need to decide for yourself if what anyone says is true. If something I say doesn't make you think, "You know, he could be right . . . I've never thought if it that way before," then I could be wrong. If I'm not bringing to consciousness things you don't already know, then don't take it from me. That could be my 20 percent.

Of course it could also be *your* 20 percent. You need to test what I'm saying against your own experiences and observations. We all need to check out the things we hear with each other— and with the Source of All Truth who guides and guards us all into truth. To "guide" doesn't mean to "coerce" or "control" or "certify"; the "guidance" of the Spirit means there is the risk of free will and thus not total safety.

On the other hand, if the things I'm saying do seem to ring true, if a light gets turned on inside you, if you find yourself thinking, "I see, I see . . ." or "Yes, that's right . . ." or "I've often suspected that but was never sure enough to say so, . . ." then it may be we're both drawing from the same source and in tune with the Source of All Truth.[15]

More than anything else, truth is recognition.[16] Edwin Muir's poem "Day and Night" speaks beautifully of things that we know "yet never have been told."[17] Jesus promised that the Holy Spirit "will teach you all things and will remind you of everything I have said to you."[18]

There are still some know-it-alls out there. Some people are like Moses—they think they can see the face of God . . .

and live.[19] The best we can do is hear God's voice and, in rare moments of mystical and metaphorical ecstasy, gently touch God's face.

What's the best thing that's going to happen during your years of education? Getting your diploma? Your degree? Making great contacts?

The greatest result of your education would be, as Socrates put it in the *Apology*, "to know that we do not know." Socrates believed that "the wise man knows that he knows nothing." On the day he died in 1988, Nobelist Richard Feynman had this saying at the top of the blackboard in his office: "What I cannot create, I do not understand."[20] Feynman was comfortable with not knowing. He once confessed to a friend, "I think it's much more interesting to live not knowing than to have answers which might be wrong."[21] Jesus' executioners were given a special pass because of their ignorance: "Father, forgive them, for they do not know what they are doing."[22] This is in fact a word of encouragement for us all, since most of the time we don't know what we are doing either.

> Jesus used to say, "I preach to you so that you may learn. I do not preach to you so that you may grow conceited."
> —Mid-9th-century Moslem scholar Ahmad ibn Hanbal[23]

WHAT WE KNOW

Even being learners, we *do* know enough to get where we're being called to go.

High up in the West Virginia mountains, where there is no light pollution, your headlights beam a straight line ahead of you, maybe six feet off the ground at most, and only a few seconds ahead of you. But you can travel across the country on that six feet of light. There's a whole big world that you can't see, yet you *can* see enough to travel from Canaan Valley to California—or around the world.

Ditto driving through life.

Philosopher Kenneth Minogue talks about those of us who suffer from "a kind of hysteria" about our ignorance—doubting our own knowledge and understanding to the extent we are unable to write a single paragraph without feeling surrounded by "abysses of ignorance." This academic disease of information overload goes by the name of the "paralysis of analysis."

Forget trying to create a magnum opus and go for the parvum opus. The epigraph in *The Captive Mind* by Czeslaw Milosz is this saying from "an old Jew of Galicia":

> When someone is 55 percent right, that's very good and there's no use wrangling. And if someone is 60 percent right, it's wonderful, it's a great luck, and let him thank God. But what's to be said about 75 percent right? Wise people say this is suspicious. Well, and what about 100 percent right? Whoever says he's 100 percent right is a fanatic, a thug, and the worst kind of rascal.[24]

Did anyone in history ever get it right the first time?

Sydney Pollack, the director of such movies as *Random Hearts, Sabrina, The Firm, Out of Africa,* and *Tootsie,* was asked in an interview, "Is there one picture you'd like to have back, to redo?" Pollock replied, "Not one—all of them! You never really get it right. That's the only reason I keep on working. Maybe one of these days I'll get it right."[25]

The pharmaceutical company Novartis has a general policy of putting money on the table for each individual on a drug development team who halts a development project. It's not a huge amount of money—just enough to act as a countering force to the natural tendency to escalate commitment to a failing course of action.

An acoustic leader both *discens* and *docens*—learns and teaches. A right spirit about learning involves confidence and humility, as does a right spirit elsewhere. We need a sense of importance—"I can do all things . . ."—and a sense of impotence—". . . without others I can do nothing."

It takes a lifetime of transformation to be led into deeper and deeper levels of truth. The older I get, the more unopened periodicals seem like still-wrapped pieces of candy. The things I don't yet know are the most delicious things of all. A professor at a ripe old age was still studying, reading, and learning as if he were a first-year student. In response to someone's "why?" he responded, "I would rather my students drink from a running stream than a stagnant pool."

> A really cultured woman, like a really cultured man, is all the simpler and less obtrusive for the knowledge.
> —Novelist George Eliot (Mary Ann Evans)[26]

The Bible says of Jesus, "The child grew to maturity and was filled with wisdom."[27]

May the same be said of us. The Jesus School is not a school we graduate from quickly. The apostle Paul himself was still learning near the end of his life: "I do not reckon myself to have got hold of it yet."[28]

SOUND CHECKS

Scientists are now "listening" for viruses by monitoring vibrations, using a quartz crystal microbalance.[29] We must do the same in our learning and in our teaching. We must monitor the vibrations.

The story is told of St. Augustine that one day as he was walking along the seashore, his mind deep in thought, his reverie was interrupted by the sight of a little boy running to the water with a seashell in his hand. The little boy filled the shell with seawater, then poured it into a hole he had made in the sand. "What are you doing, my little man?" Augustine is purported to have asked. "Oh," said the little boy, "I am trying to put the ocean in this hole."

Augustine immediately "got it." "That is what I am trying to do; I see it now. Standing on the sands of time, I am trying to get into this little finite mind, things which are infinite."

Augustine discovered something we need to remember today. We must be constantly doing sound checks—reality checks. Is what we're hearing noise or signal? Sounds are complex and confusing, often ambiguous, many times misleading. Is what I'm hearing the white-hot truth from the heavens, or is it white-noise static that obscures the truth?

A meteorite was discovered in Antarctica a few years ago. Some were convinced it came from Mars about 4 billion years ago and contains what might possibly be fossilized bacterium droppings. But while some space scientists thought they had discovered evidence of bacterial life on Mars, others thought the bacterial traces were more likely picked up while the meteorite was in Antarctica.

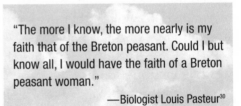

"The more I know, the more nearly is my faith that of the Breton peasant. Could I but know all, I would have the faith of a Breton peasant woman."

—Biologist Louis Pasteur[30]

How do you invest in the ears of your team? Get them hearing aids.

Hearing aids have the following component parts:

1. *Decompression chambers.* All leaders need to have a decompression chamber in which they can detox themselves: sort through all the sounds and focus on the true melody. We need to help our teams do the same: to develop their hearing, their ears.

2. *Selective hearing.* Help your team develop selective hearing. Determine together which voices to heed, which ones to marginalize. Constantly examine whether to continue to mar-

ginalize the marginalized, or to begin heeding them. Remember, hearing can be distorted; frequencies can be out of tune. We need tuning forks that have perfect pitch.

3. *Self-cleaning.* Help your team get the wax out. Learn what can be damaging to their hearing. Help them take care of their ears; don't be putting Q-tips in them! Avoid infections. Keep those ears healthy by keeping them listening to truth. Don't allow them to be distracted by the static.

4. *Hearing partners.* Give them hearing partners. Novelist Robert Musil describes one of his characters as "longing to talk, for once, to somebody with whom he could wholly agree . . . then the words are drawn out of the breast by some mysterious power and none of them misses the mark."[31]

But these hearing partners need to be drawn not just from the citadels of learning. Some of our hearing partners set the learned on their ears. Some things God has "hidden from the learned and the clever and revealed them to mere children."[32]

A man with a sprained ankle went to see his doctor. The doctor examined the ankle and told the patient to go home and soak it in hot water. The next day the man telephoned the doctor.

"Look here," he said, "I paid you forty dollars to tell me to use hot water on my ankle. I did, but it got worse. Then my house keeper told me to use cold water, and it got better. I don't understand it."

The doctor replied, "I don't understand it either. My housekeeper said to use hot water."

5. *Play.* Make learning fun. Ask stupid questions.

The Greek word for "leisure" is the word from which we get the English word "school." This is the opposite word in Greek from "business,"

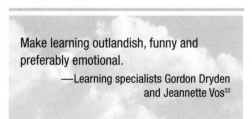

Make learning outlandish, funny and preferably emotional.

—Learning specialists Gordon Dryden and Jeannette Vos[33]

which is the negative of leisure, or *askolia*. In Latin it's the same thing: the word for leisure is *otiunt*, and the word for business is the negative form: *negotium*.[34]

In this sense, "business school" is an oxymoron.

LEARNING TO COMMUNICATE

The language of the modern world was the printed and spoken word. We have surrounded ourselves with books, newspapers, magazines, and talking-head reporters.

Postmoderns have fallen in love with the screen the way moderns fell in love with the book. They are post-Gutenberg. It's the screen that has authority, magic, and soulfulness. But media is not a zero sum game—look at the text messages on our phones.

The transition from print to multimedia does not come easily or overnight. But it's coming quickly whether we like it or not. The musical compact disc industry is bigger than the vinyl record industry it replaced; Nintendo and Sega put together are bigger than the entire motion picture industry.

> Electricity has made angels of us all.
> —Anthropologist Edmund Carpenter (colleague of Marshall McLuhan)[35]

The language of the emerging culture is sound and image—hence MTV. We live in a world of audio, video, TV, films, multimedia. Even printed text is now a digital enterprise. Literacy is needed for the reading of books. Graphicacy is needed for the interpretation of the thousands of communications that besiege us daily.

Our world is being encased in a neural net. Wiredness is what makes us seaworthy in the postmodern era.

The boundaryless environment of the Internet diminishes the control governments have over people. Communication is transactional and transnational.

In this new culture, images are central to personal life. To sculpt a metaphor is to transform the world. Good communication used to be concerned about focusing people's

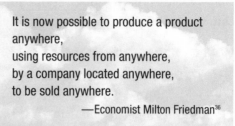

It is now possible to produce a product anywhere,
using resources from anywhere,
by a company located anywhere,
to be sold anywhere.
—Economist Milton Friedman[36]

attention so that they all "sing from the same page"; now it's about teaching people how to sequence the same monitor, how to integrate sound and print and video.

Acoustic leaders must listen to and learn from the emerging generations—their children. Listen to their fears, their hopes, their concerns. Go beyond "hearing them out." Avoid just passive "hearing," which can go in one ear and out the other. We must engage them in active listening, which requires total concentration. The listener must think alongside the speaker.

There is one thing talk *isn't* in the emerging culture: cheap. The importance of conversation is demonstrated by bookstores, which are becoming cafes to stimulate dialogue. There's a sense of urgency and passion. People see too much comfort and complacency.

"Telling stories" used to be a euphemism for lying. No more. Story is crucial in communication. Every organization needs a story—especially a compelling start-up story. Stories show the message better than we can say it.

John Raymond distinguishes between tradition-stories, map-stories, and vision-stories.[37] Tradition stories tell us where we came from. Vision stories tell us where we're going.

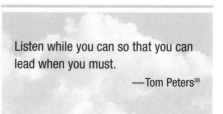

Listen while you can so that you can lead when you must.

—Tom Peters[38]

Map stories give us ideas about how to get from where we came from to where we're going. We need all those stories.

WATCHING THE COMPASS

Leaders lead by betting their lives on certain fixed points. Using a sextant, a compass, and a chronometer, a navigator can pinpoint his location by using the fixed points of the sun and the stars.

What are our fixed points today?

We need leaders with a moral compass that works full-time—and sometimes overtime.

Richard Pascale relates that "Macy's rulebook is an inch thick; Nordstrom's rules can be summed up in two sentences: Rule 1: Use your good judgment in all situations. Rule 2: There will be no additional rules."[40] Guess which company is better prepared for the future?

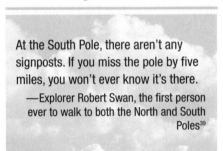

At the South Pole, there aren't any signposts. If you miss the pole by five miles, you won't ever know it's there.

—Explorer Robert Swan, the first person ever to walk to both the North and South Poles[39]

The issue is not having the Ten Commandments or Beatitudes posted on the walls of courthouses and classrooms. The issue is not to hang the Ten Commandments around the neck, but on the heart.

Dead reckoning is what a captain or navigator does in the absence of precision instruments. He looks at the information he has and makes his best determination of position from it. A lifelong learner and explorer needs to learn dead reckoning—when the texts and traditions become such a part of you that they are second nature. Acoustic leaders apply the wisdom of the ages to the soundscapes of contemporary life.

Gandhi said of the Beatitudes, "They contain a message that would save the world. What a pity that Christians have been listening to the message for two thousand years, but they [the Christians] are like stones lying in the water for centuries, never soaking up a single drop."[41]

How did John-John Kennedy end up in the water? He lost track of the horizon; he trusted his eyes and not his guidance system; he believed what his body was telling him and not what his fixed points were telling him.

At the end of Ernest Shackelton's journey, these were the only things the men returned with: historic film and photographs, a Bible, a compass and sextant, a log, and a Primus stove. And of course, the *James Caird*.

They still had their fixed points. And they made it home safely.

SHACKLETON MODULATIONS:	The Texts • The People • Clear Communication • Learning from the Past

Sounding boards can be texts or people. Shackleton was a master of both.

The Texts

Frank Worsley—the navigator—constantly pored over his navigational charts, plotting alternative routes. Shackleton did everything to protect Worsley's navigational books. These were their texts, their most precious possessions. Shackleton actually had nightmares about losing them. Without the instruments and texts, the crew would have been doomed.

The sextant, chronometer, compass, and nautical tables enabled the explorers to plot their path and position. So important was an accurate chronometer that they started out from London with 24 of them.

By the time Shackleton and five of his men set off from Elephant Island on the 22-foot *James Caird*, all Worsley had left for navigational instruments were one compass, one chronometer, one sextant, and his tables. By this time navigation had ceased being a science and had become an art form. Worsley's books soon became water-soaked and nearly worthless. He managed to take only four sightings of the sun the whole journey. But mostly by dead reckoning he got the little boat to South Georgia Island, 800 miles away!

The People

Shackleton relied heavily on the information he received from navigator Frank Worsley and the second-in command, Frank Wild. These two were the "inner core" of people he consulted. They were his main sounding boards. However, they weren't the only ones he *listened to*.

To keep up the spirits of his cold, frightened, and tearful men, Shackleton made house calls—rather, "tent calls." He engaged his men in conversation about their lives, their desires. In this way he not only kept up their spirits, but gathered valuable information about their physical and emotional states. These sound checks were vital to keeping the crew going and working together.

The Boss read his men like texts. He knew every jot and tittle of their souls; he knew which ones could live in a tent with each other; he knew which ones to take with him when he left to get help.

Shackleton kept his cool and communicated a "we're-going-to-make-it" confidence. One time when a rogue iceberg was plowing toward them, scattering everything in its path, the men began shaking hands with each other to say good-bye. They could not escape the iceberg's fury; they could do nothing but stand there and watch it come.

Shackleton calmly lit a match with his thumbnail, put a cigarette to his mouth, and smoked, watching the iceberg veer at the last minute away from them.[42] With "bring-it-on" bravado,

Shackleton taught his men to say, whatever happens, "I can learn from this" and "I will grow from this." Fear of the future was greatly diminished.

Clear Communication

Communication must address feelings and emotions, not just the reasoning mind. For postmoderns it is feeling, not thought, that must lead the way. Reason is not the highest form of human expression. Even machines are capable of reason—but they are not capable of feeling and emotion and compassion.

Marooned on an ice floe traveling three miles north a day, Shackleton drew up for each crew member a contingency plan in case of an emergency. These "orders" were written up and posted on the tents where the men were staying.[43] He knew how important it was for the men to have a purpose and a course of action. He gave all his men a voice in decisions that affected their future.

Shackleton also knew how important it was to keep a crisis edge. He responded to what he saw as a deteriorating alertness. When his marooned crewmen started barking at the cook for not customizing their orders for tea, Shackleton brought back a rationing regimen.

Not only did The Boss seek out sounding boards—he was one. He gave his crew constant feedback and immediate payback. He didn't hesitate to reward or to rebuke if necessary. However, he didn't tell them everything. Once as they rowed in the rough seas toward Elephant Island, Worsley's readings indicated that they had lost 30 miles in the winds and waves. The Boss decided it would not be wise to tell the crew the whole story. But he told them the truth: "We haven't done as well as we expected."[44]

During that race to Elephant Island, the three boats were supposed to be always in sight of each other. That became very difficult in the dark. But Shackleton was so intent on keeping communication between the boats that he came up with the idea of flashing the compass-lamp on the sails of the *James Caird* as a guide for the other boats.

On the night before he sailed away from Elephant Island with five of his men, The Boss shared his last two cigarettes with Frank Wild and gave him instructions. He wrote and signed a letter with those instructions: If Shackleton didn't return, Wild was to set off with the rest of the men in the remaining two boats and try to save themselves. Even when he was leaving, Shackleton wanted clear communication with those who remained.

Learning from the Past

Shackleton didn't believe in the notion that "you can't go back." Of course you can. You "go back" by incorporating into the present the traditions and insights of our ancestors. You learn from your own experiences and the experiences of others. You live in the present from the past forward.

Shackleton had studied his trade. An Irishman by birth, he had read sea stories from an early age. He eventually joined the merchant marine at 16, and by 26 had risen in the ranks to first mate. He learned from what he studied and what he experienced. He learned from his earlier Antarctic experiences what to do and not do.

In his "Furthest South" expedition, Shackleton had taken ponies with him to pull the sledges that carried supplies across the ice. Realizing how poorly that worked, and hearing how well the Norwegians had used sled dogs, Shackleton took dogs on the *Endurance* expedition.

Shackleton was a masterful raconteur; some called his storytelling "spell-binding." A story that Shackleton likely knew and may have told to his men involved another polar explorer of his day:

The year was 1891. The student named "Bill" had such a sharp tongue and large chip on the shoulder that he was called "Bill the Cynic." He wrote to a friend he had cut with his lashing tongue: "I know I am hard, proud, conceited, scornful, bitter ... and insulting very often, and always selfish; but I don't like you to treat me as though I wasn't trying to do a bit better."[45]

"Bill the Cynic" is known to history as Edward "Bill" Wilson, who in 1911 accompanied Robert Scott to the Antarctic and to death. While stranded in snow and storm, awaiting their death, Scott wrote of Wilson: "If this letter reaches you, Bill and I will have gone out together. We are very near it now; and I should like you to know how splendid he was at the end, everlastingly cheerful and ready to sacrifice himself for others."[46]

The expedition team called him "Bill the Peacemaker."

Wilson's trying paid off, from "Bill the Cynic" to "Bill the Peacemaker." He learned and changed.

We need to keep learning, and keep "trying to do a bit better." It takes time. But it takes.

NOTES

1. Robert Frost, "To John T. Bartlett," in Elaine Barry, *Robert Frost on Writing* (New Brunswick, NJ: Rutgers University Press, 1973), 59–60.
2. Attributed to Eric Frank Russell (using the pen name Duncan H. Monro), "U Turn," first published in *Astounding Science Fiction* (April 1950), 137. It was reprinted in *Somewhere a Voice* (New York: Ace Books, 1965), 64. While Russell did identify it as ancient Chinese, it is assumed that he did so fictitiously, as there is no evidence of any earlier use. See http://hawk.fab2.albany.edu/ sidebar/sidebar.htm. Accessed 4 April 2003.
3. Proverbs 9:10 NRSV.
4. Max Kampelman, "Democracy and Human Dignity: Political and Religious Values," *Vital Speeches of the Day* (1 June 1996), 483.
5. Eric Hoffer, *Reflections on the Human Condition* (New York: Harper & Row, 1973), 22.
6. Matthew 11:25 NJB.
7. As quoted in Denise Caruso, "The Moral Minority," *Wired* (August 2002), 72. www.wired.com/wired/archive/10.08/view.html?pg=2. Accessed 4 April 2003.
8. The words are those of Michael O'Hanlon, a defense analyst at the Brookings Institution, as quoted in Andrea Stone's "General Was 'Chosen for a Different War' But Is Adapting," *USA Today*, 1 October 2001, 8A. USATODAY .com. www.usatoday.com/news/sept11/2001/09/30/myers-usat-profile.htm. Accessed 2 May 2003.

9. George W. Bush, Radio Address to the Nation, 27 October 2001.

10. These statistics come from Clay Shirky, "Sorry, Wrong Number," *Wired* (October 2002), 097–098. www.wired.com/wired/archive/10.10/view.html?pg=2. Accessed 5 April 2003.

11. So says Joe Tucci, chief executive of EMC, one of the world's leading data storage companies. See *Trend Letter* 21 (12 August 2002), 1.

12. I am not alone. The blind writer Jorge Luis Borges (1899–1986) once said these words, which are now carved on the west wall of the award-winning Denver Public Library: "I had always imagined Paradise as a kind of library" ("Yo siempre me hab[Unknown font 1: Times New Roman CE]ía imaginado el Parad[Unknown font 1: Times New Roman CE]íso bajo el especie de una biblioteca"), "Blindness," in his *Seven Nights*, trans. Eliot Weinberger (New York: New Directions, 1984), 10.

13. Isaiah 55:8.

14. Jane Austen, *Emma* (New York: Barnes & Noble, 1996), 399.

15. Some of this is an adaptation of the foreword I wrote for Mike Slaughter's book *The Unlearning Church* (Loveland, CO: Group Publishing, 2001).

16. In her Edward Alleyn Lecture of 1944, "Towards a Christian Aesthetic," Dorothy Sayers argues that the essence of truth is recognition: "We did not know it before, but the moment the poet has shown it to us, we know that, somehow or other, we had always really known it." Reprinted in her *Christian Letters to a Post-Christian World: A Selection of Essays*, ed. Roderick Jellema (Grand Rapids: Eerdmans, 1969), 80.

17. Edwin Muir, "Day and Night," in *The Complete Poems of Edwin Muir: An Annotated Edition*, ed. Peter Butter (Aberdeen: Association for Scottish Literary Studies, 1993), 221.

18. John 14:26 NIV.

19. Exodus 33:17–23.

20. *No Ordinary Genius: The Illustrated Richard Feynman*, ed. Christopher Sykes (New York: Norton, 1994), 237.

21. As quoted in James Gleick, *Genius: The Life and Science of Richard Feynman* (New York: Vintage Books, 1992), 438.

22. Luke 23:34 NIV.

23. *The Muslim Jesus: Sayings and Stories in Islamic Literature*, ed. Tarif Khalidi (Cambridge, MA: Harvard University Press, 2001), 90.

24. Czeslaw Milosz, *The Captive Mind*, trans. Jane Zielonko (New York: Alfred A. Knopf, 1953), v.

25. As quoted in Bob Spitz, "The Ringmaster of Hollywood," *Sky* (March 2000), 73.

26. George Eliot, "Silly Novels by Lady Novelists," *Westminster Review* 66 (October 1856), 251.

27. Paraphrase of Luke 2:40.

28. Philippians 3:13 REB.

29. "Good Vibrations," *Economist* (1 September 2001), 67.

30. From Pasteur's letters to his children, as quoted in James J. Walsh, "Pasteur," *Catholic Encyclopedia* (New York: Robert Appleton, 1911), 11:537.

31. Robert Musil, *The Man without Qualities*, trans. Eithne Wilkins and Ernst Kaiser (London: Secker & Warburg, 1979), 1:257.

32. Paraphrase of Matthew 11:25.
33. Gordon Dryden and Jeannette Vos, *The Learning Revolution: A Life-long Learning Program for the World's Finest Computer: Your Amazing Brain* (Rolling Hills Estates, CA: Jalmar Press, 1994), 169.
34. With thanks to Josef Pieper, *Leisure: The Basis of Culture* (New York: New American Library, 1963), 20–21.
35. Opening words of Paul Levinson, "Telnet to the Future?" *Wired* (July 1994), 74. www.wired.com/wired/archive/2.07/future.html. Accessed 6 January 2003.
36. Friedman's exact words are, "The effect of the technological revolution has been to make it possible for a company located anywhere in the world to use resources located anywhere in the world, to produce a product anywhere in the world, to be sold anywhere in the world" (Milton Friedman, "The Second Industrial Revolution," speech to the Fraser Institute 20th Anniversary Annual General Meeting, 18 May 1994. http://oldfraser.lexi.net/publications/forum/1994/September/. Accessed 2 January 2003.
37. Conversation between author and John Raymond, associate publisher of Zondervan.
38. Tom Peters, "Rule #3: Leadership Is Confusing as Hell," *Fast Company* (March 2001), 140. www.fastcompany.com/online/44/rules.html. Accessed 29 August 2001.
39. As quoted in Curtis Sittenfeld, "Leader on the Edge," *Fast Company* (October 1999), 212. www.fastcompany.com/online/28/rswan.html. Accessed 11 May 2003.
40. Richard Tanner Pascale, *Managing on the Edge: How the Smartest Companies Use Conflict to Stay Ahead* (New York: Simon & Schuster, 1990), 64.
41. As quoted by P. J. Kavanagh, "Bywords," *TLS: Times Literary Supplement* (4 June 1999), 16.
42. Jennifer Armstrong, *Shipwreck at the Bottom of the World: The Extraordinary True Story of Shackleton and the Endurance* (New York: Crown, 1998), 74.
43. Ibid., 57.
44. Ibid., 85.
45. Letter to Mrs. E. A. Wilson found in the tent with the bodies of Scott and party. R. F. Scott, *Scott's Last Expedition* (New York: Dodd, Mead, 1913), I:410.
46. Ibid.

All Ears

*Wait for the Resonant State
and Listen to Your Inner Voice*

Your first gift is intuition.

—Artist/architect James Hubbell

Voice-activated leaders need an acute sense of timing. As you see the wave start to take shape in the distance, do you wait until it breaks to get on your surfboard? Or do you set out to meet it as it forms, and surf its crest to the shore?

The importance of timing cannot be exaggerated. Music is, in essence, an exercise in timing. Leadership requires watching and listening for things to be in a resonant state, when everything is in the right place at the right time. At that point a harmony exists between what you want to do and what can be done.

You won't always have all the data that tell you when this is. Instead, you sometimes have to trust your gut and think with your intestines.[1]

LISTENING TO THAT INNER VOICE

As you contemplate making a change, give it "the smell test." If something bothers you about it, your suspicions will often turn out to be very reliable. Trust your instincts.

Navy aviators use the word "leemers" to describe the feeling that something isn't right; and they learn to trust the "leemers."

If you try to lead by everything you've been taught about leadership, you will likely fail. At all times we must be open to the possibility that what we thought we knew is wrong. Instead, trust your gut. Intuition must be a component of decision making, especially in complex or chaotic situations, where it may be more accurate and reliable than rationalization based on past experience.

Your tendency may be to want to flip ahead in the book to see how things turn out so that you know the steps to take to solve the problem. Don't trust the process. Instead, trust the Spirit.

I'm amazed at how many church leaders listen to every other voice except that still, small voice they hear in their spir-

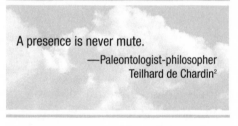

A presence is never mute.
—Paleontologist-philosopher
Teilhard de Chardin[2]

its. Call it what you want—your inner voice, your subconscious intelligence, your nondeliberative thinking. You have to make a choice to listen to that voice and move on it, or you'll push it aside or dismiss it as mere "hunch" or "instinct." These inner voices are nonrational sources of information, "learning without awareness," and can be quite sophisticated, significant, and accurate. We turn a deaf ear to them at our peril.

Voice-activated leaders choose relationship-based strategies over authority-based strategies. If you're listening, your inner voice will tell you the next step, not some authority. The inner voice is your guide and leader. Instead of depending on power relationships, depend on spirit relationships. After all, who's the best mentor in the world? The Holy Spirit, hands down.

As we sail naturally on the ocean of life, intuition is the wind. As we sail supernaturally on the ocean of life, the Holy Spirit is the wind.

How do I know some things? My deepest intuition tells me so.

Leadership listens with all senses peeled to the voice within. Learn to distinguish its pianissimo from its crescendo, the difference between its pitch that barks and the tone that purrs.[3]

One of the leading books in 1998 was *Investment Gurus*, in which the author interviewed 18 money managers and concluded that what distinguished them was their sixth sense, something you cannot define.[4]

Intuition is both a gift and a skill. Perhaps it cannot be defined, but it can be learned. Intuition is a field skill that brings together many different applications: the rationality of breaking things down and analyzing component parts, the imagination of putting the whole back together again, the semiotics of pattern recognition and assumption making, the discernment of the "greater thans" in the sum of a whole's parts.

The U.S. Marines now include intuitive decision making as an important part of their training. They have run into problems with the rationalistic planning and strategic-analysis models. Thus the official Marine Corps policy reads as follows: "The intuitive approach is more appropriate for the vast majority of ... decisions made in the fluid, rapidly changing conditions of war, when time and uncertainty are critical factors, and creativity is a desirable trait."

This doesn't mean you totally give up your brain for your gut. You still need to learn and listen, but

> The tigers of wrath are wiser than the horses of instruction.
> —Mystic-poet William Blake on the way intuition beats out analysis and theory[5]

when it comes down to that tough decision, trust your intuition. Bow your head to your heart. It's what sets you apart from a machine.

Machines tend to act rationally and predictably. But any behavioral economist will tell you that people don't. The world doesn't revolve around rationality and predictability. Be willing to trust your inner voice, the voice that Isaiah 30:21 talks about when it says, "Whether you turn to the right or to the left, your ears will hear a voice behind you, saying, 'This is the way; walk in it'" (NIV).

How do you keep your bearings? In the modern world it was through "common sense." In the postmodern world it's "uncommon sense."

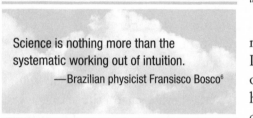

Science is nothing more than the systematic working out of intuition.
—Brazilian physicist Fransisco Bosco[6]

No organization needs a CIO, or Chief Intuition Officer. Every organization needs to help *every* person become a CIO.

About Intuition

What intelligence enables swallows and terns to pinpoint their way across planet Earth? To call someone "bird-brained" seems almost a compliment.

Even "bird-brained" humans have the apparatus to be intuitive, says neuropsychiatrist Mona Lisa Schultz. She defines intuition as "the ability to make a correct decision with insufficient information."[7] It's a normal part of perception, but a part that we have denied and blocked.

There are differing skills and powers of intuition. Anyone can play the piano (that is, use one finger to tap out a tune), but not everyone can become a Mozart. It's the same with intuition. According to researchers of intuition, being in the receiving mode for the wisdom of the world is key to activating the skill.[8] Everything that exists is trying to speak. Leaders learn to translate and sometimes speak the language of the universe, the "music of the spheres."

Francisco Varella and Claire Petitmengin-Peugeot at the Institut Nationale des Telecommunications in Paris studied intuition and reported their findings in the *Journal of Consciousness.*[9] They found "an established succession of very precise interior gestures with a surprising regularity from one experience to another and from one subject to another." They discovered this intuitive pattern:

1. "Gesture of Letting Go"—slowing down of mental activity, and "deep rooting, or interior self-collecting."
2. "Gesture of Connection"—linkage with the object of the intuition; sometimes literally by touching, sometimes visceral, mental, etc.
3. "Gesture of Listening."
4. "Pre-Intuition"—call it an "empty passage," or "moment of confusion," or "silence" preceding the intuition. "The intuition can surge forth as an image, a kinesthetic feeling, a sound, a word, or even a taste or an odor, most often in several simultaneous or successive forms."[10]

Intuition can go wrong. The invention of psychotherapy was an intuitive leap. Sigmund Freud wrote to Carl Jung and admitted that "my whole makeup is intuitive."[11] It was Freud's "intuitive" impressions that led him to argue that sexuality was the source of the religious impulse.[12] But reason can go just as wrong as intuition.

> The true organ of thinking is not the head but the heart.
>
> —Ancient Chinese saying

Resonance

Think about the power of resonance: a small sound can resonate into something larger. Small inputs can result in huge consequences. A lot of little inputs can cause mountains to collapse. In self-organizing dynamical systems, small micro-scale fluctuations can have macro-scale consequences.

But not if the timing is off. A sense of timing is critical. You can push and push on a tree as it's being cut down, with no result. But when the cut gets to that certain stage—that tipping point or threshold—suddenly a little push can bring the tree crashing down. You have to rock at the right frequency to calm crying infants (one cycle per second); otherwise they keep crying.

The rate of change in our culture is accelerating exponentially. We have already talked about the changes that have taken place in a single lifetime and about the fast pace of technology. And if you think speed and competition are tough in your field, think about this: In 2002, at Chicagoland Speedway, Sam Hornish beat Al Unser Jr. by .0024 seconds while traveling at speeds approaching 200 mph! That's 2.4 one-thousandths of a second.

How do animals navigate? Through dead reckoning. And dead reckoning requires a highly sensitive sense of time. The culture of speed that we live in makes a leader's sense of timing all the more essential. That is why we need to trust the One who is beyond time. The One who is always with us. The One who speaks to us in that "still, small voice."

> May you have the hindsight to know where you've been, the foresight to know where you're going, and the insight to know when you've gone too far.
>
> —Old Irish toast

In the Celtic fishing villages of Connemara, there is a little phrase that says, "*Is fánach an áit a gheobfá gliomach*"—that is, "It is in the unexpected or neglected place that you will find the lobster."[13]

Irish poet John O'Donohue interprets this saying to mean, "In the neglected crevices and corners of your evaded solitude, you will find the treasure that you have always sought elsewhere. Ezra Pound said something similar about beauty: Beauty likes to keep away from the public glare. It likes to find a neglected or abandoned place."[14]

Beauty likes neglected places.

Sastrugi are wind-blown waves or ridges in the snow. They follow the prevailing winds. At one point in crossing the barren Antarctic snow, Ernest Shackleton reportedly "steered by the sastrugi."[15] He knew which way the wind was blowing, and which way he needed to go. By using the relationship between the two, he was able to guide the land party in the right direction.

Maybe there are times when the prevailing wind needs to be followed. More often you may need to go the opposite direction, or even crosswise to the winds. But whatever way you need to go, you first have to know which way the wind is blowing.

You can look at it in two ways:

> An accurate statement of the problem is about 100% of the solution.
> —*Danish poet-scientist-philosopher Piet Hein*

Or,

> When your cart reaches the foot of the mountain, a path will appear.
> —*Old Chinese proverb*

I go with the latter.

Sabbatical

With our tight schedules and our long work days, few people seem to get enough rest today. We rush from one thing to another, even working at our play. We end up with

> If the Lord had not been on our side . . .
> the flood would have engulfed us,
> the torrent would have swept over us.
> —Psalm 124:2–4 NIV

"hurry sickness," which bumps our timing off. We complain about our hurriedness and are less productive because of it.

The more we step up and step out, the more we need to get out of step. The more we move at the speed of light, the more we need to travel at the speed of sound. There is a relationship between content and time: certain kinds of content require more amounts of time.[16] The most time-intensive content today just happens to be the most highly valued skills in the 21st-century: relationships, intuition, creativity, communication, collaboration, critical reasoning, continuous learning.

Time is life's fundamental necessity but has become the ultimate luxury—the most expensive and extravagant thing we have. We're in a time famine; we don't need more free time as much as we need more time that is free from desires and demands. No matter what we may think, technology doesn't so much give us more time as enable us to do many more things in the time that we have. In addition, technology makes us more enslaved to work, not less. You don't have to walk far on a crowded beach to find someone busy at a laptop.

What we need is more sabbaticals—time to learn and explore the secrets of the soul. I am not talking about the "year-off-for-research-and-study" type of sabbatical. I am talking about mini-sabbaticals that are skinny-dips in the fountain of youth.

There are three important s's for sabbaticals: stillness, silence, and saying no.

Music encompasses and embraces silence though it is made of sound. The rests are what make notes possible. It's the same with life. We need lots of time with nothing to do. Souls are drawn to stillness the way objects are drawn to the ground, the way sounds are drawn to silence.

One company, Alette & Associates, offers a Napping Nook. Another company, PCI Services, offers its employees two nap rooms with recliners, cots, and earplugs. They have discovered that a 20-minute nap gets people 3–4 more hours of productive work time.

Sometimes you need to pause to reveal to yourself whether you need to rev up or calm down, whether you feel stuck, sucked in, or stuck up.

New Wastebaskets

Are you bringing great things to life? Then you are bringing some things to death. What are

> I have found God's address. It is at the end of my rope.
>
> —Dallas Willard

you rendering extinct? Extinction is an integral part of renewal. In fact, the only alternative to extinction is biological stagnation.[17] The real question is whether you will focus on a sense of loss or an anticipation of what is to come.

With computers has come a new kind of "trash can" (or "recycle bin"). It's a place where we can dump things without really getting rid of them. Until we "Empty Recycle Bin," we can always go back and retrieve whatever we dumped there. We need the same thing in life: places to toss things and leave them for a while before deciding what to do with them—extinction or emergence.

In the modern era we criticized writers and others for not being fond enough of their wastepaper baskets. Physical and spiritual houses of the emerging era will feature compost drawers and recycling bins, but there will still need to be wastebaskets. However, they will not be the kind of "waste" baskets of the past.

"Waste" is not the dirty word we have made it out to be. If an activity is not "useful," we say it is a "waste of time." Watching *The Bear* (1989) or *Fantasia* (2000) is absolutely useless and an utter waste of time—but what a worthwhile waste of time!

When you pray or meditate, you are "wasting time," as the modern world defined wasting time. You aren't getting anything done. But spiritual "wasted" time—the disposals of prayer, meditation, praise, confession, Bible study—is our best use of time.

What if we went through life never wasting time? "Think how severely we should be judged," Jesuit priest James V. Schaal reminds us, "if we never did a thing that was not simply useless! We would literally go through life doing nothing for its own sake."[18]

Even God "wasted" time. "On the seventh day God rested and drew breath," the Bible says.[19]

In baseball we have the seventh-inning stretch.

Downtime is necessary for creativity and intuition. For the incubation of reflections and relationships. For God to work in our minds and hearts. For us to hear the song inside us. The creative mind, while in the act of creation, is like a fading coal. It's a battle requiring both industriousness and indulgence to keep something alive that is constantly flagging and wanting to go out.

> Because I have loved so deeply,
> Because I have loved so long,
> God in his great compassion
> Gave me the gift of song.
> —Singer-pianist Nina Simone[20]

Waste space is most particularly God's space—the space God enters most readily. Look at all that empty, wasted space in Gothic cathedrals. But that was God's space. Look at all the empty, wasted space in one's life going to concerts and plays. But that is God's space. Poet Laureate Andrew Motion, in his prologue poem "The Dancing Hippo," shows how our equation of waste and uselessness do not go together:

I know, it was useless, of course, her dancing.
I know. Like everything else we do. But God above
it was beautiful. God![21]

Time off, wasted time, or useless time is often God's time.

The faster life goes, the slower you need to get. In order to keep many balls in the air, you have to let them all down sometime. We all need time to download, boot, and reboot.

Incubation time is necessary for imagination. Rest is a requisite for any action that can outpace and outrace.

Harmony

Some people talk about achieving "balance" in life. But "harmony" is a better metaphor than balance. I can never expect to live a balanced life, but I can expect to live a harmonious life, in which the ends are held in tension or harnessed, not leveled out.

Elizabeth Gibson-Meier, a senior consultant at RHR International Company, doesn't believe in balance. Instead, she contends that life entails dealing with variables. We all face different situations, different variables. One person's solution may not work for the next person. We can't just "balance" life by deciding how much time or energy we must devote to certain parts of our lives. We must regularly ask ourselves the question, "How much is enough?"[22]

The first thing God sanctified was not a place or a person or a thing, but a time: Sabbath time. We need Sabbath time more now than ever.

We have as a Pilot one who sleeps in the back of boats.

When "nothing" is happening, something is happening. The technical term for silence should not be "dead air," but "live air."

When water is still, it becomes clear. So, too, the mind and soul.

SHACKLETON MODULATIONS:	Keeping Sharp • Supreme Intuition • Waiting for the Resonant State • A Fourth Presence

Ernest Shackleton knew the importance of keeping the mind sharp. He knew that if his men lost their focus and quit tuning in to each other, they would have chaos, perhaps anarchy, and certain failure. So The Boss took care of his men.

Keeping Sharp

Shackleton wanted the crew to get exercise. On the ice floes he encouraged the men to play soccer or whatever other sport they chose. He also believed in parties, and he actually allowed pigs on board for future pork roasts.

The dogs that had been brought along for pulling sleds were assigned to certain men for their care. Those men trained and bonded with those dogs and in this maintained a real sense of purpose.

Shackleton encouraged laughter among his crew; and he encouraged the practical jokes others played as long as they weren't demeaning or didn't present a danger.

The men found all kinds of ways to entertain themselves during the dark months of the Antarctic winter. They had dogsled races. They played cards and other games, listened to records on the gramophone, and read aloud to each other. They did impersonations and gave lectures on topics in which individuals had particular expertise. Frank Worsley taught some of them a Maori war dance. Even Shackleton was not averse to embarrassing himself for the sake of his crew's morale: He competed in—and won by a landslide—a worst-singer contest! The crew conducted trials for fun, during one of which Worsley was charged with stealing a button from an offering plate in church.[23]

Beyond the mock trials were mock lectures, mock sermons; mock recitals; mock costume parties—all designed to help keep the men in a good frame of mind, to give them little "sabbaticals" from the stress of survival.

Supreme Intuition

Every leader needs a reputation as something of a conjurer, a magician with a bag of tricks. Shackleton never revealed

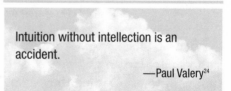

Intuition without intellection is an accident.

—Paul Valery[24]

all his secrets, but there was purpose behind everything he did. He was known as having a sixth sense for being "present" in an emergency.

The path through the ice was never a straight one. It took intuition to feel one's way forward into the open ice through the Antarctic Circle. Choices were never clear-cut. Shackelton had to listen to his inner voice and choose the right timing each step of the way. And he was seldom wrong—never wrong enough to lose one of his men.

Shackleton saw *mirabile dictu* everywhere. He had a wonderful gift of being able to see everything as if for the first time. No matter how prosaic or desperate, he found all human experience interesting—and tried to make it so for his men.

Waiting for the Resonant State

Upon reaching South Georgia Island, having traversed 800 miles of the roughest seas in the world and having landed on a narrow little island, Shackleton still had to cross a terrain that no man had yet crossed to get to the whaling station on the other side of the island. They had chosen to land on the south side of the island because they deemed it too dangerous to attempt to land on the north side, where prevailing winds might just blow them right past the island and out to sea.

After 17 days in the *James Caird*, all six men were on the verge of total physical exhaustion. Living in the cramped, cold quarters of the small boat had taken its toll. The six still had not reached safety, and the remainder of the crew were still stranded on Elephant Island. With 29 miles to go across the island's razorback ridges and glaciers to reach the whaling station, Shackleton would have liked to press on. But he knew his crew needed rest to get well. So he declared a sabbatical. They found a cave with "a curtain of enormous icicles screening the entrance" where they started a fire. There they could get their feet dry and get the blood circulating again. They ate and slept. Ate and slept. For days.

The time came to complete their journey to civilization. The mountains of South Georgia were the Alps of Southern Ocean. They were uncharted and menacing. No one had ever crossed them on foot before. But Shackleton saw no other option.

They couldn't come all this way and be stopped by a mere 29 miles.

Three of them—Shackleton, Worsley and Crean—set off, with Worsley still the navigator. Formidable peaks, cliffs, and glaciers appeared in every direction. And in the midst of them lay vast fields of snow-covered ice. It was not an encouraging sight for the already weary threesome.[25]

A Fourth Presence

Because of their exhaustion and numbness, Shackleton declared 15 minutes of walking to be followed by a two-minute sabbatical. As the three men trudged along, each began to sense a peculiar feeling—something none of them dared share until later.

They all felt that there was a fourth person with them. Worsley even wrote later that as they journeyed, he would count Shackleton, Crean, and himself, and then in his mind wonder who the fourth was. He knew there wasn't really a fourth person, but all of them felt that presence. In thinking back on the experience, all three of them had to stop themselves from saying there were four crossing the mountain together.[26]

Reflecting later on the whole journey, Shackleton observed, "When I look back at those days, I do not doubt that Providence guided us, not only across those snowfields, but also across the stormy white sea. . . . I know that during that long march of thirty-six hours over the unnamed mountains and glaciers of South Georgia it often seemed to me that we were four, not three."[27]

What got them through? Intuition . . . and that mysterious
Fourth Presence.

NOTES

1. Thomas A. Stewart, "How to Think with Your Gut," *Business 2.0* (November
   2002), 99–104. www.business2.com/articles/mag/0,1640,44584,00.html.
   Accessed 11 May 2003.
2. As quoted by Dare Morgan, Jesuit spiritual director at the El Ritiro San Iñigo
   Retreat Center, Los Altos, California. www.elretiro.org/About/about_sd_mor-
   gan.html. Accessed 21 May 2003.
3. This is a distinction developed by the poet Geoffrey Hill that refers to the
   construction of words and their relationship to a poet and his or her audi-
   ence.
4. Peter J. Tanous, *Investment Gurus: A Road Map to Wealth from the World's Best
   Money Managers* (New York: New York Institute of Finance, 1997), 374.
5. William Blake, "Proverbs of Hell," in *The Marriage of Heaven and Hell, Repro-
   duced in Facsimile* (New York: E. P. Dutton, 1927), 9.
6. As quoted by Emilios Bouratinos, "Consciousness and the Snare of Civilisa-
   tion: A Reappraisal of Human Evolution," *Network: The Scientific and Medical
   Network Review* 72 (April 2000), 2. Scientific and Medical Network,
   www.datadiwan.de/SciMedNet/library/articlesN71+/N72consciousness_Bou
   ratinos.htm. Accessed 19 May 2003.
7. Mona Lisa Schulz, *Awakening Intuition: Using Your Mind-Body Network for
   Insight and Healing* (New York: Harmony Books, 1998), 19. Schulz writes,
   "Intuition is just another sense, like seeing or feeling or hearing. Moreover, it
   is a sense we all share. We are all intuitive" (2).
8. "Subjects report that 'it is given to me.'" See Claire Petitmengin-Peugeot,
   "Anatomy of an Intuition: A Scientific Study Reveals What Intuition Looks
   Like and How to Encourage It," *Spirituality & Health* (Winter 2000), 45. See
   also Penney Peirce, author of the book *The Intuitive Way:* "You may be sur-
   prised how much guidance you receive when you believe in the wisdom of
   the world," as quoted in Alison Rose Levy, "Can You . . . Should You . . . Do
   You . . . Trust Your Intuition," *Spirituality & Health* (Winter 2000), 44.
   www.spiritualityhealth.com/newsh/items/article/item_117.html. Accessed
   13 May 2003.
9. Petitmengin-Peugeot, "The Intuitive Experience," 43–77.
10. Ibid., 45.
11. As quoted by Lesley Chamberlain in *The Secret Artist: A Close Reading of Sig-
    mund Freud* (New York: Seven Stories Press, 2001), 63.
12. See Sigmund Freud, *Totem and Taboo: Some Points of Agreement between the
    Mental Lives of Savages and Neurotics* (New York: Norton, 1950) and *The
    Future of an Illusion* (New York: Liveright, 1928). For a backlash against "intu-
    ition" in some religious circles, see Jeff M. Sellers, "The Higher Self Gets
    Down to Business," *Christianity Today* (February 2003), 36, which argues that
    "intuition" (along with "transformation" and "interconnectedness") is a code
    word for New Age spirituality.

13. John O'Donohue, *Anam Cara: A Book of Celtic Wisdom* (New York: Cliff Street Books, 1997), 103.
14. Ibid.
15. Roland Huntford, *Shackleton* (New York: Atheneum, 1986), 107.
16. This is why some people, such as Noam Chomsky and Edward Said, now refuse to be interviewed on television: they will not be given the time to explain a concept to the end.
17. See Michael Boulter, *Extinction: Evolution and the End of Man* (New York: Columbia University Press, 2002).
18. James V. Schall, *Unexpected Meditations Late in the Twentieth Century* (Chicago: Franciscan Herald Press, 1985), 131.
19. Paraphrase of Genesis 2:2.
20. Frontispiece to Philip Wexler, *Holy Sparks: Social Theory, Education and Religion* (New York: St. Martin's Press, 1996), iii.
21. Andrew Motion, *Natural Causes* (London: Chatto and Windus, 1987), 12.
22. Elizabeth Gibson-Meier, as quoted by Eric Ransdell in "The Consultant" *Fast Company* (July-August 1999), 154. www.fastcompany.com/online/26/consultant.html. Accessed 12 March 2001.
23. Jennifer Armstrong, *Shipwreck at the Bottom of the World: The Extraordinary True Story of Shackleton and the Endurance* (New York: Crown, 1998), 33–34.
24. Paul Valery, "Odds and Ends," in his *Analects*, trans. Stuart Gilbert (Princeton, NJ: Princeton University Press, 1970), 34.
25. Ernest Shackleton, *South: The Story of Shackleton's 1914–1917 Expedition* (London: Heinemann, 1970), 112.
26. Armstrong, *Shipwreck at the Bottom of the World*, 110.
27. Shackleton, *South: The Story of Shackleton's 1914–1917 Expedition*, 125.

In One Ear, Out the Other

Monitor the Background Noise and Unleash Creativity

chapter 7

> The most gifted members of the human species are at their creative best when they cannot have their way.
>
> —Philosopher Eric Hoffer

Einstein was once asked what the difference was between him and the average person. He said that if you asked the average person to find a needle in a haystack, the person would stop when he or she found a needle. He, on the other hand, would tear through the entire haystack looking for all possible needles.

The English word *noise* comes from the Latin for "nausea," which means seasickness. Today too much information buzz, or "noise," is making people sick. If you are a pastor, you know what I mean. Everyone is screaming for your attention.

But noise can make you healthy as well as sick. Like Ezekiel's winged lion, the sound of whose wings was like a great torrent or cloudburst, "noise is the interference that is simultaneously disruptive and creative," writes Mark Taylor. "The interplay of noise, which is informative, and information, which is noisy, creates the conditions for emerging complexity, which is the pulse of life."[1] Complexity is "the property of being able to react to noise in two opposed ways without ceasing to function," states Henri Atlan, a biophysicist at the University of Paris.[2]

MONITORING THE NOISE LEVEL

Because there is so much noise invading the lives of church leaders, the tendency is to try to escape the noise. We build "sound barriers" that keep the noise at a distance. For life to work, for self-organizing systems to function, there must be neither too little nor too much noise. But the worst-case scenario of all is no noise, a condition that many of us seek by staying in our offices, forwarding the phone, and zoning out during meetings.

Effective leaders cannot tune out the noise that surrounds and confounds us. We need to listen to—and through—it.

In the business world, people are starting to talk about how to listen "musically," not just critically. Leaders need to listen to the undertones of conversations, the underlying resonances of words and phrases and tones of voices, the beneath-the-surface meanings of what people are saying and how they are saying it.[3]

People can distinguish 500,000 different sounds, but it takes a discerning ear to sort out what we need to hear. Think of "noise" as any potential distraction and you begin to understand the challenge today's leaders face. How do you lead in such an environment?

Part of the problem is that we don't know what we want. It's hard to listen for the right things. One minute we want a savior; the next minute we want a scapegoat. In this emerging culture, "leader" and "lead" (as in bullets) have become synonymous.

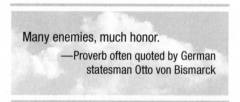

Many enemies, much honor.

—Proverb often quoted by German statesman Otto von Bismarck

One of the ways leaders try to tune out the noise is to hang out only with those who are solid allies. I hope we are honest enough to admit that even in the church culture, a leader will have detractors. *Enemies* may be too strong a word, but there's a lesson to be learned from Mafia don Michael Corleone in *The Godfather: Part 2* (1974): "Keep your friends close, and your enemies closer." You always want to keep your ear tuned to those who would like to see you fail, perhaps even more than to those who want to see you succeed.

A mark of a great leader is the ability to hear and honor those who would dethrone him. In the shark-infested waters of life, "swim with the sharks,"[4] as one author puts it, not just with the dolphins.

Leaders who avoid conflict and swim only with the friendly are depriving themselves of an opportunity to learn.

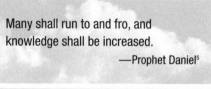

Many shall run to and fro, and knowledge shall be increased.
—Prophet Daniel[5]

You do not have to like the sounds that come from your detractors, but if you tune into the messages behind the sound, you will be a more effective leader.

But to turn your cheek doesn't mean you turn your back.

LEARNING FOR THE FUTURE

Part of the problem in trying to lead in a "noisy" environment is that we live in a world where changes are happening so fast that it's almost impossible to give good directions. If we aren't careful, our instructions will turn out to be like those of the old farmer who said, "Turn at the corner where the old Johnson farm used to be."

Doing anything today—life, business, relationships—is like building a tower over a fault line. To be an effective leader, you need to be able to take in new facts, confront new realities, and not be scared.

Careers of the future will be based much less on progressing through an organization's hierarchy (after all, there won't be many hierarchies left) than on progressing through many different project assignments that develop an individual's marketable skills. In this environment, intellectual capital is the most important resource for sustained effectiveness, and creativity stands out as the best way to leverage intellectual capital.

As Charles Exley, former CEO of NCR, admitted to his staff, "I've been in this business 36 years and I've learned a lot—and most of it doesn't apply anymore."[6]

Do you have a lesson plan for unlearning the information that will just stand in your way?

One of the harsher realities for church leaders is that experience is no longer an asset. And that idea runs counter to everything you have been taught about leadership. The "seasoned" leader, the myth goes, is more capable of leading effectively than the inexperienced. But experience actually handicaps you. No "experience" can prepare you for the challenges ahead. In fact, "experience" often leaves you in the dark. Too many church leaders are relying on strategies, methods, information, and systems that are so outdated as to be barriers to leadership. The tried and true was true when it was tried. It may be false today.

In this new world, *the way* we learn is as important as *what* we learn. Lecture-drill-test education doesn't cut it. Our children's minds are already wired differently from ours because of all the technology that's been part of their lives since birth. Now we're seeing the start of Virtual Learning, where virtual reality is a new learning tool. This changes the course of how children learn even more.

Our children don't learn the important things by reading a book and spouting facts back on a test. They actually function like scientists—coming up with ideas about how things work and then trying them out. They test what happens around them, both in the world of things and the world of ideas. As they figure things out, they hone their thoughts to better connect with reality. Jean Piaget was not the first and will not be the last to point out that children don't learn just through lessons in classrooms, but through interacting with whatever they contact in the environment around them.[7]

Playing is the best path to learning. Is this how you are learning?

Sadly, most pastors and church leaders look back at their seminary years as the last time of real intellectual engagement. What's most sad about that is the fact that what they learned may have even been outdated at the time. If you are not fully engaged in a program of continuing education, you cannot possibly lead a congregation who most likely is.

It doesn't have to be a formal program at a local university. In fact, there's no need for that anymore. Check out the *Electric Library* at *www.elibrary.com*. It makes available thousands of articles and transcripts. Opposed to paying for full access to a website? Remember how valuable information is?

The Peter Drucker Foundation is a virtual foundation. In the words of its chair, Frances Hesselbein, "We have no money. We deal in intellectual capital."[8]

Leaders who operate intellectually at less than full bore will be left bankrupt. What's your lesson plan—or your business plan—for learning?

At the same time, just surfing the Internet haphazardly isn't the answer. It has lots of noise that is absolutely useless, even harmful. The old southern saying is still true: "Buzzard's nests seldom hatch eagles." Be careful what you put into your mind. And what you encourage others to put into theirs. Learning is the principal means of value creation, so make sure the "values" you are creating are honorable and edifying.

The more "virtual" the organism, the more informal and flexible the management system, the more values must become central and fixed. As a leader you have a great opportunity to help shape the lives of learners. Do it together. Shift from a "teacher-teaching" model to a "learner-learning" model. If learning isn't taking place, neither is teaching.

Also, take every opportunity to celebrate knowledge activities. Create knowledge symbols (a kind of *status* symbol?) and signals for your people; encourage attendance at continuing education events. Reward those who bring back and share knowledge; offer unstructured time for knowledge gathering.

It's been said that books have become cigars for the brain. People don't read as much as they used to, but Daisy Maryles, executive editor of *Publishers Weekly* since 1986, notes that "people want to read something they view as significant or trendy or that people are talking about." Liquor companies have even started sponsoring literary evenings where readers can mingle with authors.[9] Could the church do that better?

What I am talking about is not so much the time-honored tradition of Christian education, but a mindset toward learning that you model for your staff and those who look to you for leadership. Sunday school isn't enough anymore. Learning is a full-time endeavor.

We all need our fix of data; we all need to feel that blast of information. The Internet provides unbelievable (sometimes literally so) resources for learning. But we also need the high-impact learning of experience and interaction with other people over issues of relevance. Sometimes the distance learning is shown to be invalid by the up close, and vice versa. The key is to combine the far distant and the up close. We need both.

INTREPID INNOVATION

Creativity can be found in the background noise. Innovation can grow out of what's discovered there.

Don't expect the church to support innovation. Almost all big, old organizations are naturally resistant to change. Think about how hard it is to move that old piano. Most people who innovate do so "in spite of" the powers-that-be, not because of them. Capitalism is lauded as the best economic system for generating growth precisely because of its ability to produce a continuous stream of successful innovations, whether garage innovation (lone entrepreneurs) or "routinized" innovation of large firms (more important long-term).[10]

Don't give in to the tyranny of "either-or," teeter-totter thinking. There's more than one way to skin a . . . trout. Stephen Jay Gould argued that there are structures of the human brain still in place from Paleozoic (that is, fish) times called "atavistic" forms of behavior. One of the chief of these atavisms is our penchant for "or" thinking— thinking in dichotomies, dividing people up into "them" and "us,"[11] sheep and goats, enemies and friends, East and West. According to Gary Hamel, "When you hear 'or,' it's an invitation to innovation."[12]

> The crowd doesn't recognize a leader until he is gone; then they build a monument for him with the stones they threw at him in life.
> —J. Oswald Sanders in *Spiritual Leadership*

The late Edwin Friedman once proposed that all institutions who fund research projects should set aside 5 to 10 percent of their monies for projects that totally contradict those projects they have chosen to fund. Only in this way, he argued, can the human race "prevent its knowledge from keeping it from learning more."[13]

Could you imagine the church doing the same thing?

Inside every successful organization there is a musical score for innovation. And every score has three key musicians: the composer (the idea person), the conductor (the creative people and others who believe in the idea and put their reputation on the line for it) and the orchestra (the people who actually implement the idea and make it better). Without all three, there will be no true innovation, and little success. Innovation is a communal, not an individual enterprise. When "time is money," it pays for innovators to share their knowledge, and innovation spreads rapidly.

A caution here. Innovation is not technology. Innovation is knowledge of the culture one is in and the management of that knowledge. Innovation is getting the culture right. Innovation is not harnessing resources or harnessing products but harnessing knowledge. That's why innovation is a matter of life-and-death.

Innovation is less a matter of designating certain people as "CKOs" (Chief Knowledge Officers) than a matter of training each person to be a CKO. Leaders and organizations need to grow new knowledge and spread it throughout the organism.

What is your plan for growing new knowledge of your church, its community, and the world in which each of your members live? If you're operating on a demographic profile of your community that was commissioned two years ago, it's already ancient. Why? The world changes drastically every 18 months. I have a friend who thinks I'm much too conservative. "The world changes every nine months," he insists. The newest data says that the world has generated more information in the past 3 years than in the previous 5000 years. There's so much information out there that we need to make sure we're focusing on the information that really matters.

Political scientist Michael Nelson is known for digging deep into the relationship between the presidency and the press, getting beyond surface relationships. He defends his approach by pointing to the oceanographer. Most of us look at the ocean in terms of the waves on top. They're what we can see. The oceanographer looks instead at the vast majority of the ocean that is unseen. Though the waves are more visible and perhaps more interesting at first, they are not representative of the ocean itself. And the ocean itself is what the oceanographer wants to study.[14]

Nothing fails like success: it freezes you in patterns that brought you success 12 months ago but that will bring you failure today. Most churches are operating with information about how things were years ago.

UNLEASHED CREATIVITY

What is the most creative thing you've done as a leader? What is the most creative thing your church or organization has done in the last year?

The old way of thinking is that leaders must encourage and manage creativity. The new leader will embolden and empower creativity. As much "context-provider" as "content-provider," the leader creates an environment around the team that nourishes and nurtures creativity. This doesn't mean pampering creative people or catering to their whims. What it does mean is finding ways to get rid of obstacles that get in their way. It means getting out of their way so they can do what they can do best.

> The most successful man in life is the man who has the best information.
>
> —Benjamin Disraeli

Think workspace doesn't matter? Consider this comment by innovation expert Gerald Haman, on "Cubicle creativity": "The size of their ideas is directly proportional to the space they have in which to think."[15] They're limited by the box they are in. Maybe "out of the box" really means getting your people physically out of their constrictive environments. What would happen if your next staff meeting took place on the fifty yard line of a football stadium? Too hard to manage?

Creative people often thrive on challenge. You will find that difficulty is an aid to creativity: "A difficulty is a light; an insuperable difficulty is a sun," wrote French poet Paul Valéry.[16]

As sleep guru-physician Martin Moore-Ede reminds us, "The power of your brain—creativity—counts more than the size of your forearms."[17]

Here are the Four Horsemen of the Apocalypse of Noncreativity. These are certain creativity killers:

1. Criticism
2. A team of like
3. A team which only praises success
4. Bad space

See any problems with your management style and creativity? With the type of team you've chosen? With your attitude toward success? With your physical space?

The leader needs to be open to the creative ideas of people around him. History has not shown that to be a prevalent attitude:

Luther rejected Copernicus.

J. P. Morgan turned away William C. Durant's proposal for financing an upstart automobile company, then called International Motors. It's now called General Motors.

How many times have you seen a bias toward the rich and famous rather than the inspired and original?

The postmodern world is not an industrial era, but a creative era where life forms can be reconstructed and reinvented. The Internet enables one little ma-and-pa store in Iowa to sell to millions of people; the only thing standing in its way is lack of creativity.

In this world, true leaders exhibit courage, endurance, confidence, and humility. Their task is getting people to face up to the truth, to see the realities and challenges that are around them. Once people realize the truth, the leader's job is to help people tack into those challenges and make them work for the team's benefit.

Eighty-nine percent of 150 executives surveyed in 1999 said their firms have made dramatic progress in the past five years in encouraging employee creativity and innovation.[18] Some are truly changing. Others have a long way to go.

Where are you? Where is your church?

Leaders sometimes convince themselves that things are going well because they are in control. However, what really makes things go well is the relationship between the leader and the led. If a leader thinks he or she has all the answers, you can be sure that the people being led realize that's not true. Admitting the truth builds relationships, and relationships get results.

Community in postmodern culture is not dependent on a "point person," but on the connection, the relationship. Leadership involves an unspoken contract:

> Leadership is not about the leader. Leadership also includes those who are led. It is the followers who place one of their own in a position of leadership, even if they do so only by agreeing to follow. A leader with no followers is no leader.[19]

SHACKLETON MODULATIONS: | Ready for the Future • Sorting through the Noise

Ernest Shackleton was a master of monitoring the noise for valuable information. He was a great listener and a great discerner of what he heard. In addition, he knew just when to encourage creativity and when to demand compliance.

Ready for the Future

Shackleton had been on an Antarctic expedition on which many got sick because of inadequate nutrition. He didn't want that happening on his watch. So he consulted a British army nutritionist who claimed people needed certain vitamins in their diet—a new concept at that time.

Shackleton decided to take along a supply of rations developed by this nutritionist that were designed to provide what the men needed for long days of travel on the ice. These rations were made up of animal fat, beef and vegetable proteins, oatmeal, sugar, and salt. The rations were formed into blocks weighing half a pound, enough for one meal. Each one contained almost 3000 calories, and they could be boiled in water to make a thick green-pealike soup. The result was a food source that gave balanced nutrition and helped prevent scurvy. Scurvy was the plague of sailors on long journeys, and it was at least partially the cause of Captain Scott's death.[20]

Also before embarking for Antarctica, Shackelton and his men spent a month at South Georgia Island, where they sat at the feet of the Norwegian whalers and station managers. They studied the conditions of the ocean and picked the brains of the only people in the world who truly knew firsthand the waters and ice they would be facing. Shackleton wanted to be as knowledgeable and mentally prepared as possible. He gathered information that later turned out to be of inestimable value in the survival effort.

The Boss also encouraged innovation in preparation for what was to come. He knew that the crew would eventually have to depend on the lifeboats to get them to safety. So during the long months of waiting on the ice, he had Harry McNeish, the ship's carpenter, take advantage of available lumber salvaged from the *Endurance* to beef up the lifeboats. McNeish added taller sides on the biggest boat ("whale-backs"), making her more seaworthy and allowing her to carry more. He also devised better ways to keep water from coming in over the sides, and he created shelter for supplies stored in the bottom of the boat. These enhancements proved immensely valuable on the *James Caird's* 800-mile journey from Elephant Island to South Georgia Island, navigating the roughest seas in the world.[21]

Sorting through the Noise

After *Endurance* was crushed, and after the celebrations for Christmas in 1915, Shackleton and his crew left Ocean Camp, hauling the two boats across the ice at night. Presumably the surface would be harder at night, but it proved to still be soft. The men's boots filled with seven pounds of freezing water with each step. The ice conditions also made it nearly impossible to push or pull the lifeboats, which were loaded with supplies.

After the crew had made little progress in three days, McNeish, the oldest but strongest member of the crew, refused to budge any further. The era of wooden sailing ships reserved a special status for carpenters. In the navy they were "warrant officers." In the merchant service they got their own cabin and were called "idlers" because they didn't have to stand watches. Carpenters were a pampered, independent sort.

British naval law released a ship's crew from its obligation to the captain when a ship was lost. No longer were the crew members required to do the duties assigned aboard ship, and no longer would they get paid. McNeish knew all this, and he was determined that it applied to the *Endurance* expedition. Beyond the borders meant no more orders. He didn't intend to follow orders from anyone.[22]

Shackleton saw MacNeish's attitude as mutiny, betrayal. He also knew what a perilous state the men were in. His monitoring of the noise revealed broken hearts, broken backs, and a university crew nearly at the mental breaking point. He retrieved the ship's crew list, which he had saved, and read the Ship's Articles, which each man had signed before leaving England. Shackleton had customized the contract to fit this journey, and he read this section aloud to his men:

> All members of the Crew without exception to have interchangeable duties. . . . The Crew agree to conduct themselves in an orderly, faithful, honest, and sober manner, and to be at all times diligent in their respective Duties, and to be obedient to the lawful commands of the said Master . . . whether on board, in boats, or on shore.[23]

Technically they were now on shore, and to disobey the commands of the master would be punishable by law. They would continue to be paid, and the Ship's Articles were still in effect. No one took McNeish's side, and the mutiny was short-circuited.

Shackleton then took McNeish aside and spoke with him privately. The Boss made a point not to embarrass McNeish in front of the rest, but surely reminded him that execution is the punishment for mutiny.

The next night McNeish was at his post when the command was given to move on. However, after that night—including incidents in which feet broke through thin ice—Shackleton made the decision to retreat to a solid, safer floe and to wait out the trip north on the ice. The Boss hadn't ignored the noise he'd heard loud and clear.

Here is Shackleton's version of "keep your friends close and your enemies closer": "Keep malcontents close to you and win their support." The more conflicted the personality, the more Shackleton made you his confidant. The more tempestuous your temper, the more likely you were to share The Boss's tent. He did all he could to win you over. Once you were called on the carpet, you didn't have a tough time getting off it. But he faced reality courageously. When it came to the 800-mile lifeboat journey, Shackleton selected to go with him on the *James Caird* five men. Two were chosen—McNeish and John Vincent—because they were troublemakers, and Shackleton wanted to keep them close to him rather than let them loose among those left behind on Elephant Island.

You can't destroy your enemy without destroying yourself.

NOTES

1. Mark C. Taylor, *The Moment of Complexity: Emerging Network Culture* (Chicago: University of Chicago Press, 2002), 121, 123.
2. As quoted in ibid., 137.
3. Ronald Heifetz, "The Leader of the Future," *Fast Company* (June 1999), 130. www.fastcompany.com/magazine/25/heifetz.html. Accessed 25 May 2003. See also the later development in Ronald Heifetz and Marty Linsky, *Leadership on the Line: Staying Alive through the Dangers of Leading* (Boston: Harvard Business School Press, 2002), 64-67.
4. Harvey Mackay, *Swim with the Sharks: Without Being Eaten Alive: Outsell, Outmanage, Outmotivate, and Outnegotiate Your Competition* (New York: Morrow, 1988).
5. Daniel 12:4 KJV.
6. Charles Exley, as quoted in John R. Wilke, "NCR Is Revamping Its Computer Lines in Wrenching Change," *Wall Street Journal* (20 June 1990), A1.
7. So argues Neil Gershenfeld in *When Things Start to Think* (New York: Henry Holt, 1999), 138.

8. As quoted in "The Drucker Foundation for Nonprofit Management Profile," *Philanthropy News Digest* 6 (25 January 2000). http://fdncenter.org/pnd/archives/20000125/003142.html. Accessed 12 May 2003.

9. Walter Kirn, "Rediscovering the Joy of Text." *Time* (21 April 1997), 104. www.time.com/time/archive/preview/from_search/0,10987,1101970421-137565,00.html. Accessed 22 November 2003.

10. This is the thesis of Princeton economist William Baumol in *The Free-Market Innovation Machine: Analysing the Growth Miracle of Capitalism* (Princeton, NJ: Princeton University Press, 2002).

11. John R. G. Turner, "Life on the Hardwire," *TLS: Times Literary Supplement* (27 September 2002), 10.

12. Gary Hamel, "Innovation Now!" *Fast Company* (December 2002), 121. www.fastcompany.com/online/65/innovation.html. Accessed 11 May 2003.

13. Edwin H. Friedman, "Maps," a speech delivered at the 1983 meeting of the American Family Therapy Association, as later transcribed in an issue of *AFTA Newsletter* [n.d.], 9, which is available from the American Family Therapy Academy, 2020 Pennsylvania Avenue NW, #273, Washington DC 20026.

14. Michael Nelson, "Why the Media Loves Presidents: And the Presidents Hate the Media," *Vital Speeches of the Day* 65 (15 June 1999): 541.

15. Gerald "Solutionman" Haman, founder of SolutionPeople in Chicago, as quoted in Mary E. Morrison, "New! Improved! Creating and Marketing New Products Demands the Kind of Insights that Kellogg Delivers," *Kellogg World Alumni Magazine* [Kellogg School of Management, Northwestern University], Winter 2001. www.kellogg.nwu.edu/kwo/win01/indepth/new.htm. Accessed 25 May 2003.

16. As quoted in Iris Murdoch, *The Book and the Brotherhood* (New York: Viking, 1988), 581.

17. As quoted in Anna Muoio, "Are You Sure You're Up for the 24-Hour Economy," *Fast Company* (October 1999), 72. www.fastcompany.com/magazine/28/24hour.html. Accessed 21 May 2003. The quote begins, "You might be able to shovel coal or bend steel while your brain is operating at half capacity, but. . . ."

18. As reported in "Help Wanted: Creative Thinkers," *The Futurist* (August-September 1999), 2.

19. Mark Ernsberger (president and CEO of Farr Associates), "Leadership: It is Not for the Faint of Heart," *Vital Speeches of the Day* 66 (1 June 2000), 511.

20. Jennifer Armstrong, *Shipwreck at the Bottom of the World: The Extraordinary True Story of Shackleton and the Endurance* (New York: Crown, 1998), 8.

21. Harding McGregor Dunnett, *Shackleton's Boat: The Story of the James Caird* (Benenden, Kent: Neville & Harding, 1996), 21.

22. Armstrong, *Shipwreck at the Bottom of the World*, 63.

23. Ibid., 64.

chapter 8

Modulate

*Preparedness
over Planning*

> You have an idea, and then you just put one dumb foot
> in front of the other and course-correct as you go.
>
> —Media mogul Barry Diller[1]

When you "musick," you perform, listen to, compose, or dance with music. Something happens when musicians musick together, something as ineffable as a mystical experience. Musicking is more than a "special effect."

The church has always had music. What it has lacked is leaders who know how to musick.

MUSICKING MODULATIONS

Conductor Leonard Bernstein talked about so letting the music flow and so identifying with the composer "you *become* that composer."[2] At times Bernstein lost sense of himself as a separate composer when conducting. Jazz trumpet players tell of the sensation of becoming a trumpet. Singer-composer Neil Young talks of this out-of-body experience of transcendent consciousness as going "through the wall":

> [You] hit the wall . . . it's the *end of notes*. It's the other side, where there's only tone, sound, ambience, landscape, earthquakes, pictures, fireworks, the sky opening, buildings falling, subways collapsing. . . . When you go through the wall . . . it

doesn't translate the way other music translates. . . . I love to
go through the wall.³

When selfhood is transcended and ego loss is achieved, one
enters a group experience of consonance and harmonic relationships. Would you describe your relationship with your staff
or congregation as that kind of a group experience?
It could be you're spending too much time planning and
not enough time preparing.
The planning mode leads to dissonance. The modulation
mode leads to consonance. The challenge of voice-activated
leadership is to move from the planning mode to the modulation mode, to move from dissonance to consonance, from lin-
ear thinking to lateral thinking. In modern times we focused on
salvation through processes and planning. Any action must
come out of a "long range" plan that establishes long-term goals
and objectives. Before any concrete steps are taken there must
be a "strategic plan" and, behind it, "action plans" and "backup
plans." Our view of the future was based on "feasibility studies" and the plans we controlled (or at least thought we did).
There is no evidence that "planning" yields a brighter
tomorrow. Never has. Never will. Ask any gardener, who will
tell you that whatever you plan, it doesn't turn out the way you
intended it. That's why voice-activated leaders focus on the
modulation mode, which is less a rowing motion than surfing
action, less a feasibility study than a faith stance. The modulation mode is based on unpredictability, letting people swim in
"new streams" and "have their head," admitting the impossibil-
ity of control.⁴ It means letting the music flow—playing music
without scores, building structures without blueprints, taking
journeys without maps.
Modulation means replacing "plans" with metaphors and
songlines of preparedness. Modulation means replacing a philosophy of "results" (production, sales, cash flow, net profit,

membership gains, budget increases) with a philosophy of "resonance," where power and success reside not in rank or position but in relations and being. Success is not self-authenticating.

"There is no time lost in preparation." My mother taught my two brothers and me this almost as a litany of life. Even Jesus spent time in the desert, preparing himself for what he was to face. He didn't plan his future; he prepared for it.

What's wrong with refusing to go into the future without a Triptik?

Wrong Plot

First, there's a wrong plot. We want to know how something will work out before we get into it. But that's not possible. We *don't* know! Life is not rationally ordered. We can't plan for the future because we can't predict the future. We can no more predict the future than we can foretell the forever after. We can no more know how this day will end than we can know the end of our days. "Sometimes—there's God—so quickly," says Blanche DuBois in *A Streetcar Named Desire.*[5]

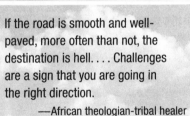

If the road is smooth and well-paved, more often than not, the destination is hell. . . . Challenges are a sign that you are going in the right direction.

—African theologian-tribal healer Malidoma Patrice Somé

It is in the nature of life to "break in"—to surprise us, startle us, come upon us suddenly, even vigorously. "Crisis management" is an utter oxymoron like "risk management." The peace of stability is another name for the peace of the grave. Nothing is stable around us anymore. Status quo means death; perpetual innovation and change is life.

What organism plans its life? What person can plan his or her future? Can you plan your love? Can you plan your relationships? Can you plan your passion? Have you ever tried "thinking straight" and "planning ahead" in your love life?

Anything alive and vital doesn't plan its way forward, but prophesies its way forward. It lives its way forward and modulates according to what happens. All structures are processes of energy, processions of activities.

We live in a world of radical indeterminacy and acute uncertainty. In this world of volatility, leaders need sight-reading and sigh-reading abilities. They need to be willing to see when something isn't working and adapt so that it does work. Or kill the whole thing and start over.

Robert Young is a veteran of three start-ups, the founder of Red Hat and of Lulu Press, a peer-to-peer publishing experiment aimed at academia. Young says that the only thing you can predict in a start-up is that revenue comes from where you least expect it. "I have yet to be in a start-up that was successful doing what it set out to do," he says. "An executive too focused on the original business plan generally misses the bigger opportunity."[6]

It may be nice to have a fixed sense of the order of things. But how often do the things we plan in life work out just the way we planned them? Do you make lists? Have you ever gotten one day to go according to plan?

It's like sailing. We're headed toward a certain destination, but first we have to tack in one direction and then another to get where we are going. And that doesn't include the times when the wind blows us off course or we go in a new direction entirely.

Who made it to the top of Everest first? In 1953, Sir Edmund Hillary and Tenzing Norgay became the first on record to reach the summit. Did mountaineers George Mallory and Andrew Irvine ever make it?

The "controversy" was stirred when the body of Mallory, who disappeared in 1924 near the top of Mount Everest, was found in 1999 at 27,200 feet. Did Mallory and Irvine die on the way *to* the summit or on the return? No one knows for sure.

Responding to the controversy, Hillary has said, "The point of climbing Everest should not be just to reach the summit. I'm rather inclined to think that maybe it's quite important, the getting down." Hillary and his expedition were able to adapt and complete their mission. Mallory and Irvine did not.[7]

Hillary and Norgay remain the first to reach the summit and make it down alive.

Life is false to formula. There are only two safe predictions about life. First, life will be certain to press upon us questions we never thought of before; it will present us with issues we never even dreamed

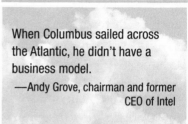

When Columbus sailed across the Atlantic, he didn't have a business model.

—Andy Grove, chairman and former CEO of Intel

existed. Second, as John Lennon penned in the song "Beautiful Boy," "Life is just what happens to you, / While you're busy making other plans."[8]

We need to stop worrying about planning and spend more time preparing. Then we will be ready to modulate when things don't go the way we expected them to. Instead of using the planning mode, leaders prepare for the future by "rehearsing" a variety of scenarios and possible modulations.[9] When the Central Command of the U.S. military argues that it doesn't need to change its master plan in the Iraq War because "our Master Plan has built-in preparations for any and all eventualities," it is not operating out of a mechanical "planning" mindset but a dynamic "preparedness" mindset. Intuition comes to those who are prepared.

Much of life happens spontaneously. Werner Heisenberg's "Uncertainty Principle" describes the incomprehensible mystery at the center of creation. No system behaves in a totally predictable manner. Leaders recognize the limits of our knowledge about everything. In our world, planning is worse than a mistake—it's an evil.

During World War II, Gen. Douglas MacArthur called in one of his army engineers and asked, "How long will it take to throw a bridge across the river?"

"Three days," the engineer told him.

"Good!" said the general. "Have your draftsmen make drawings right away."

Three days later, the general sent for the engineer and asked how the bridge was coming along. "It's all ready," replied the engineer. "You can send

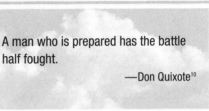

A man who is prepared has the battle half fought.

—Don Quixote[10]

your troops across right now, that is if you don't have to wait for the plans. They aren't done yet."

Think of how rapidly your church could be mobilized for ministry if it didn't have to wait for the plans.

Wrong Pilot

The second thing wrong with the planning model is that the wrong pilot is at the helm, a wrong planner called the "self." We want to pilot our own lives.

We expect to self-pilot our way into the future. The hyphenated self was the pride and joy of modernity—self-help, self-power, self-service—but it was also the end of wisdom and wonder. The harder we work at controlling our environment, the more we feel that we are less and less on top of things than ever before. Because we are.

Self-control may be the ultimate sin—wanting the self to control life, or controlling the self so that the self can control life. That's why we jog and jazzercize like mad to stave off being out of control over our aging, sagging bodies. That's why we run to any quack we can find when we've been told there's nothing more that medicine can do—we can't stand not being in control of our destiny. That's also why we keep checking our email and our cell phone messages. We don't want anything to take us by surprise and knock us out of control. If we can manage to think of ourselves as being in control of life and can work at manipulating everything from that perspective, it makes us happy. That's why so many people lead self-centered, miserable lives.

It's time to let out the reins—to decontrol ourselves. Twelve-Step programs work because one of the first things they do is force the addict to realize he is not in control of life. Addicts are forced to open their eyes and ears to wider horizons, including the acceptance of a Higher Power and the fact that they are powerless on their own.

Isn't it a bit ironic that an addict accepts a Higher Power while many of us in the church are reluctant to release our grip on self-power?

Learn to let go. Listen for the harmonious vibrations (the "eurythmics") around you. Lean into life. Trust the creative forces of the universe.

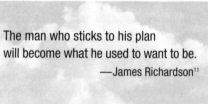

The man who sticks to his plan will become what he used to want to be.
—James Richardson[11]

These may seem like scary concepts in your orderly organization, but they are mandatory for soundful leaders.

Wrong Propulsion System

The third thing wrong with the planning model is its propulsion system. Planning is akin to the workings of an internal combustion engine: fuel funnels through tiny openings into sealed compartments, where controlled explosions are ignited—if everything is working right. Meetings are the control pipeline that channels special interests into the right compartments and keeps the energy of divergent ideas and idea-makers from exploding in our faces.

What if, instead, we were able to catch and ride the tailwinds of these idea-makers' powerful energies? What if we harnessed that energy to drive our structures? What if we allowed ourselves to be "played," to become an instrument in the hands of the wind, where one's words and actions strike chords that produce a heart song? No special interest or diverse constituency is without glimpses of truth, or without the potential of a heralding cry that can awaken us to receive the future. It's up to us to discern the spirits, monitor the messages, discriminate between poseur and prophet, and hear the chimes of the times.

All structures tend toward automatization—where functions become unthinking, reflexive, and automatic. Every structure needs periodic de-automatization. The heralding cries voicing diverse songs must be allowed to grip our attention, focus our minds, and warn us of destructive patterns.

So how far and fast will this new propulsion system propel us? We'll find out along the way. But first we must relax, celebrate, and let go of our need to control all ideas and idea-makers. We must pray and play with them, and learn from their emperor's-new-clothes kind of authentic analysis. We must trust the whole-making and Holy Spirit to make our people a communifying force. They, like we, are not the point of it all, but rather a piece of it all.

Mountains and valleys are brief sojourns. We don't live in them; we just pass through them. Creation is to be enjoyed.[12]

ADJUSTING AND ADAPTING

Ever try to guide a cat or a puppy? No one steers a living thing; it simply takes one step at a time. No living enterprise moves forward by "planning." The same goes for self-organizing systems. Instead, they reveal: "We made it up as we went along."

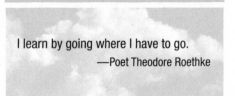

I learn by going where I have to go.
—Poet Theodore Roethke

When you come to a pothole, you don't need a strategic plan to get by it. You improvise. After a brief moment of panic, you ad-lib your zigzags until you regain your bearings. It's not planning strategies that get you down life's potholed or bouldered streets, but improvisational strategies.

The skill of modulating involves learning to adjust to any situation, identifying the adaptive challenges, and adopting an adaptive temperament, exquisitely calibrated to the moment. It's the ability to spot the unexpected and then adapt to meet its challenges.

Take the way George Lucas says he makes a movie. He approaches a film in the manner a Victorian carpenter approached the building of a house—not with any preconceived blueprint or plan, but with an openness to the creative flow and the shape the house itself wanted to take. No wonder Victorian homes are so wonderfully full of mysterious nooks, twisting corridors, and rambling outhouses.

Name a successful company that has followed a master plan to success. Starbucks morphed and modulated into success. Kinko's evolved to where it is today.

Have you heard of "the Yanahaira Crisis"? From 1956 to 1961, Professor Isaku Yanahaira was one of the portrait sitters for the Swiss artist Alberto Giacometti. One afternoon, in mid-sitting, Giacometti's hand was holding the brush and he was about to paint a stroke. Suddenly his hand fell, "as if repelled by the canvas." He tried again, and again it fell. Time after time he tried to paint a stroke on the canvas, and each time his hand fell.

When he realized he could not paint one stroke, he held his head in his hands and wept. He cried for ten minutes. He cried, he said later, because he realized that what was he was attempting to do was beyond his reach. "Your head is like a bomb," he told Professor Yanahaira. "If I touch it, I shall destroy everything . . . my life."

At that moment Giacometti's painting took a new turn. "Until this point I was hoping to make a picture of your

> Drawing is nothing more than taking a line for a walk.
>
> —Swiss artist Paul Klee

head," he told Yanahaira. "I now paint to see where the painting will take me."[13]

Giacometti thereafter always said that he painted "to see where the painting will take me."

FLUIDITY FOR THE FUTURE

Think about the Ark and the Titanic. Why did one float and the other sink? One was built by an amateur, the other by professionals. One had elaborate blueprints and huge specs; the other was intuited and revealed. One was built in the backyard, the other in a shipyard. One was built to withstand the unknown; the other tripped over the experience of its builders— they built it to withstand what they thought they knew.

Our "arks" need to be built for the conditions we're facing, conditions we know we don't know: the utter and complete discombobulation of the future. An ark is built for the dark.

Maybe amateurs have an advantage over professionals. They don't have the "light" of experience and the training that are no longer valid in our world. An amateur doesn't know the "right" way to build it. An amateur is not confined by the guidelines of the guild. An amateur resists the lesson-drawing impulses of the past.

We're used to mainlandized, mainlined, "landlubber" leaders. But our world has moved from fixed to flexibility to fluidity. We need leaders who can do the same thing—adapt to the changing conditions and lead in new ways. Twenty-first-century leaders have moved from the sylvan days of the status quo to the seasick days of the "fluxus quo."

If chaos is really "an archetype of novelty, creativity, innovation, and surprise,"[14] as Ralph Stacey suggests, where is your life most creative and innovative right now?

The modern era's bias against "water" is evident in our language. To say someone is "all wet" was not a compliment. It was very bad to be "over your head" or "out of your depth."

> Yonder is the sea, great and wide,
> creeping things innumerable are there,
> living things both small and great.
> There go the ships,
> and Leviathan that you formed to
> sport in it.
>
> —The Psalmist[15]

Water covers two-thirds of our planet's surface; it comprises 65 percent of our bodies. The average USAmerican uses 80 to 100 gallons per day to stay clean and healthy. The number one requirement for being one of the 100 world-class super-cities of this century is having a more than adequate supply of water, "the oil of the 21st century."[16]

Everything fixed is becoming fluid. If we don't adapt . . . we'll drown.

THE GREATEST OF THESE

Our postmodern times are bringing the "downfall of the barracudas, sharks, and piranhas and the ascendancy of nice, smart people with a passion for what they do."[17]

Is love merely a 4-million-year-old four-year itch? Is love more than an unrestrainable and irrational rush of phenylethylamine (an amphetamine-related compound)?

Philosopher Milton Mayeroff, author of the book *On Caring*, defines love as "the selfless promotion of the growth of the other."[18]

Love is the ultimate "killer app," argues a Yahoo senior executive in *Fast Company*. The winners are the great lovers.

The most powerful force in business isn't greed, fear, or even the raw energy of unbridled competition. The most powerful force in business is love. It's what will help your company grow and become stronger. It's what will propel your career forward. It's what will give you a sense of meaning and satisfaction in your work, which will help you do your *best* work.[20]

> Love and the hope of love,
> friendship, books, the joy of art,
>   good Scotch
> even the random sporting event—
>   these constitute
> the white cane that keeps us
>   tapping forward into
> the dark.
>
> —Poet Stephen Dobyns[19]

Faith is the art of hearing the invisible.
Hope is the art of believing the invisible.
Love is the art of trusting the invisible.

SHACKLETON MODULATIONS:	Improvisation • Love for His Crew

Ernest Shackleton loved the lure of Antarctica: "I have ideals," he said, "and far away, in my own white South, I open my arms to the romance of it all." However, Shackleton never knew what the bag of Aeolus would bring him: sunbeams, snowflakes, cloudbursts, hailstones.[21] What it did bring him was some of the worst weather on the planet.

Improvisation

"A man must shape himself to a new mark directly the old one goes," Shackleton wrote in his diary when his dreams were shattered along with the *Endurance* as it was crushed by the ice.[22] Shackleton didn't have a precise plan for the journey. Instead, he was great at improvising. He didn't function according to elaborate, detailed plans, but would "play it by ear" as he went along. He made sure he had equipment, supplies, and a good crew, and then was confident he could figure out what to do no matter what difficulties arose.[23] He proceeded, not with a plan, but with a dream and a hope. He moved ahead with a stoic determination to look forward, not back.

The Boss lead his team uniquely for the time. He involved his men in decision making, which was unheard of at that time for a strong leader. He allowed his men a long leash in their areas of specialization. He encouraged adaptation and creativity.

Six dog-teams had been brought along for the overland journey. When the *Endurance* got trapped in the ice, some of the crew constructed "dogloos" on the ice alongside the ship. They came to call the little settlement "Dog Town." Shackleton's men were encouraged to express their own creativity as they built the dogloos, giving them steeples, porches, and other fanciful architectural features.

At Ocean Camp there were five canvas tents to house 28 members of the crew. The group of men in each tent was given the freedom to be creative in making their accommodations as dry and cozy as possible.

Shackelton's confidence never waned—at least not as far as anyone noticed. He seemed to be at his best when contriving experiences to keep his men from losing hope. He devised a variety of competitions, sing-a-longs. and entertaining evenings that diverted the crew's attention from their desperate situation. His own energy and confidence rubbed off on the crew, and eventually they, too, believed they could conquer any adversaries they faced.[24] Just because there may be no answer, Shackleton insisted, doesn't mean there is no hope.

As the months of waiting on the ice wore on, Shackleton and his men kept trying new things. Even with blistered and frostbitten hands, they kept active. Even when they lost feeling in their toes from waterlogged boots, they kept active. Even when they moved just an iota and ice cracked from their clothes, they kept active. Even when they were struggling with diarrhea, they kept active. Saltwater boils on their faces broke open and pus froze on their frostbite, and yet, when they were more dead than alive, they spotted the "snow-covered basalt peaks of Elephant Island" thirty miles ahead.[25]

Love for His Crew

Shackleton's biggest fear when the crew members were in the lifeboats on the open sea was that the three boats and the men would become separated. He wasn't interested in surviving himself if all his men didn't survive as well. Even when the nearly unseaworthy lifeboat *Stancomb Wills* slowed them down to the point of a dangerous crawl, there was no talk of abandoning some that others might live. The best ship, *James Caird*, was lashed to the worst, and the lead was then assumed by the second ship, the *Dudley Docker*.

When Ernest Holness, enclosed in his sleeping bag, slipped into a yawning crack in the ice, it was The Boss who reached into the freezing water and threw him back on the ice just before it closed its jaws. When the ice floe they were on cracked while they were trying to warm up Holness, everyone jumped to safety before Shackleton. By the time it was his turn to jump, the expanse of water was too wide. The men watched him disappear into the mist until one of them launched a rescue boat to bring him back.

Shackleton's men related later how those few minutes with The Boss drifting away in the darkness were some of the most frightening moments they had ever experienced.[26] When everyone was safely back together, Shackleton's first thoughts were not of himself but of fireman Holness. "You all right, Holness?" Shackleton asked the man who was still in danger of freezing to death. He was more concerned about the well-being of one of his men who was at risk than he was about the near-miss he himself had just experienced.

The lowest on the pecking order was the stowaway, Perce Blackborrow. He was the youngest man on the expedition, having hidden on the ship until it was too late to take him back. In the long months that had passed, Blackborrow had become a true member of the crew. Nearing the end of the journey, however, he suffered severe frostbite. By the time the three lifeboats were approaching Elephant Island, he had no feeling left in his feet. When it became apparent to Shackleton that they would set foot on land the next day, he called out Blackborrow's name. When the man responded weakly, Shackleton announced that he, Blackborrow, would have the honor of being the first to go ashore where no one had ever landed before.[27]

Sure enough, two of the crew helped Blackborrow, who couldn't walk, be the first onto shore. The last shall be first.

On the *James Caird*, in the midst of the miserable 17-day, 800-mile voyage, Shackleton kept a close eye on his companions. When in the frigid and dreadfully wet conditions someone seemed to be weakening, Shackleton would call for a break and demand hot milk for everyone. That way the man who really needed the warmth and nourishment would receive it, but no one would be embarrassed by being singled out. And everyone would be stronger for the task that remained.[28]

As the *James Caird* approached South Georgia Island, a hurricane took hold of the boat, and the crew fought it for nine hours. The same hurricane sank a 500-ton steamer from Buenos Aires, with all hands lost. Waves crashed against the *James Caird;* the crew couldn't try to land or they would be smashed against the rocks. When the winds finally subsided, they made it ashore. After 18 months in the Antarctic, the men were back on South Georgia Island—but on the wrong side of the island and with swollen and frostbitten legs.

On the grueling 36-hour, almost nonstop journey across the uncharted mountains of South Georgia, Shackleton could think of little else but his men stranded on Elephant Island. He realized that without their fate motivating him, it would have been easy to give up and let sleep quilt his pain and puzzlement. But being the leader he was, Shackleton knew he had to keep going. He later described how he continually thought about getting his men to safety:

> That was the thought which sailed us through the hurricane and tugged us up and down those mountains . . . and when we got to the whaling station, it was the thought of those comrades which made us so mad with joy that the reactions beats all effort to describe it. We didn't so much feel that [they] were safe as that they were saved.[29]

When you're close to death every day, life becomes more precious. You sort out what's important and what's not important.

The ultimate in musicianship? In the words of poet Patrick Kavanagh, it is "to play a true note on a dead slack string."[30] The story of Sir Ernest Shackleton's expedition aboard the *Endurance* has been called "the greatest survival story in all of history." And Shackleton may have been one of the greatest leaders of all times.

Most important to him—and his keynote of virtue—he kept his promise: He brought all his men back alive.

NOTES

1. As quoted in Polly LeBarre, D Day for the Techno-Elite," *Fast Company* (August 2003), 42. www.fastcompany.com/magazine/73/dispatches1.html. Accessed 22 November 2003.
2. As quoted in William L. Benzon, *Beethoven's Anvil: Music in Mind and Culture* (New York: Basic Books, 2001), 10.
3. As quoted in ibid., 144–45.
4. Even William B. Rouse, known as one of the top "planning" consultants in the world, has argued that "plans" should be seen, not as "road maps" that you follow religiously, but "maps" that "place you in the path or, better yet, at the crossroads of serendipity." See William B. Rouse, *Best Laid Plans* (Old Tappan, NJ: Prentice Hall PTR, 1994), 206.
5. The concluding line of scene 6 in Tennessee Williams, *A Streetcar Named Desire*, in his *Four Plays* (London: Secker & Warburg, 1957), 121.
6. As quoted in Michael Learmonth, "The Open Source Ringmaster," *Wired* (December 2002), 040. www.wired.com/wired/archive/10.12/start.html?pg=5.

7. Tim Friend, "Body on Everest May Be 1924 Explorer Who Sought Summit," *USA Today* (4 May 1999), 8D.

8. John Lennon, "Beautiful Boy," Capitol/EMI Records, 1980.

9. Henry Mintzberg, *The Rise and Fall of Strategic Planning: Reconceiving Roles for Planning, Plans, Planners* (New York: Free Press, 1994), 248–52.

10. Literal translation of *"Hombre opercebido, medio combatido,"* in Miguel de Cervantes Saavedra, *The Ingenious Gentleman Don Quixote de la Mancha,* trans. Samuel Putnam (New York: Viking, 1949), 2:611.

11. James Richardson, *Vectors: Aphorisms and Ten-Second Essays* (Keene, NY: Ausable Press, 2001), 73.

12. See my "A Survival Guide for the Third Millennium: What Potter A. Qoyawayma Taught Me about Spiritual Leadership," *Soul Cafe* 2 (October-November 1996). www.leonardsweet.com/sweetened/Editions/v2n6-7.html. Accessed 29 May 2003.

13. See the essay by Sachiko Natsume-Dube of Osaka University about "the Yanahaira Crisis," as presented first to a symposium held at the Sainsbury Centre. For more on Yanahaira and Giacometti, see Reinhold Hohl, *Alberto Giacometti* (New York: Harry N. Abrams, 1971), 171–74, 281, and an article in *Art News* (January 1962), 41–57.

14. Ralph D. Stacey, *Complexity and Creativity in Organizations* (San Francisco: Berrett-Koehler, 1996), 60.

15. Psalm 14:25–26 NRSV.

16. McKinley Conway, "The Great Cities of the Future," *The Futurist* (June-July 1999), 28. USAmerican candidates are Atlanta, Dallas, Denver, Phoenix, Seattle, Portland, Salt Lake City, Honolulu, Orlando, New Orleans. Around the world the candidates include Madrid, Melbourne, São Paulo, Toronto, Guadalajara, Lyons, Stuttgart, Shanghai, etc.

17. Tim Sanders, "Love Is the Killer App," *Fast Company* (February 2002), 64. www.fastcompany.com/magazine/55/love.html. Accessed 14 February 2004.

18. These oft-quoted words of Mayeroff's are frequently attributed to *On Caring,* but they do not appear in the book: Milton Mayeroff, *On Caring* (New York: Harper & Row, 1971).

19. Stephen Dobyns, "Bead Curtain" in *Common Carnage* (Newcastle upon Tyne: Bloodaxe, 1998), 29.

20. Sanders, "Love Is the Killer App," 66.

21. In Greek mythology Aeolus, the god of the winds, helped Odysseus on his sea journey by fastening the unfavorable winds in a leather bag that was not to be opened. But once while Odysseus was sleeping, his sailors, believing that the bag contained a secret treasure, opened it, and the ship was blown back to its starting point.

22. Shackleton's diary entry as quoted in granddaughter Alexandra Shackleton's foreword to Kim Heacox, *Shackleton: The Antarctic Challenge* (Washington, DC: National Geographic, 1999), 7.

23. Jennifer Armstrong, *Shipwreck at the Bottom of the World: The Extraordinary True Story of Shackleton and the Endurance* (New York: Crown, 1998), 9.

24. Harding McGregor Dunnett, *Shackleton's Boat: The Story of the James Caird* (Benenden, Kent: Neville & Harding, 1996), 42.

25. Armstrong, *Shipwreck at the Bottom of the World*, 86.
26. Ibid., 80.
27. Ibid., 88.
28. Ibid., 100.
29. Ibid., 116.
30. Patrick Kavanagh, *Self-Portrait* (Dublin: Dolmen, 1964), 29.